# THE RAGDOLL REVERIE CAT

*A comprehensive guide to raising, loving, training and understanding the world's affectionate cat*

# Table of contents

Introduction
CHAPTER 1
    RAGDOLL CATS – A UNIQUE AND WONDERFUL BREED
        Physical Characteristics
        Temperament and Behavior
        Reaching Full Maturity
        Is a Ragdoll Cat Right for You?
CHAPTER 2
    HISTORY OF THE RAGDOLL CAT
        The Origins of the Ragdoll
        Ragdoll Myths and Truths
        The Modern Ragdoll Cat
CHAPTER 3
    PURCHASING A RAGDOLL CAT
        Buying vs. Adopting
        Rescues and Shelters
            Local Shelters
            Local animal shelters often have a variety of cats available for adoption, including purebred Ragdolls and Ragdoll mixes. While finding a Ragdoll at a general shelter might require more patience and persistence, it's not uncommon. Checking online databases, such as Petfinder or Adopt-a-Pet, can help you locate Ragdolls in shelters near you.

- Breed-Specific Rescue Networks
- Tips for Adoption

## CHAPTER 4
### ALL ABOUT RAGDOLL BREEDERS
- Finding a Reputable Breeder
- Health Tests and Certifications
- Breeder Contracts and Guarantees
- Choosing Your Perfect Kitten
- Adopting Multiple Cats

## CHAPTER 5
### PREPARING FOR YOUR RAGDOLL CAT
- Necessary Supplies
- Preparing Your Other Pets
- Preparing Your Children and Family
- Kitten-Proofing Your Home
- The First Few Weeks

## CHAPTER 6
### CARING FOR YOUR RAGDOLL CAT
- Indoor or Outdoor
- Emotional Needs
- Hairballs
- Enrichment and Playtime

## CHAPTER 7
### TRAINING AND SOCIALIZATION
- The Importance of Socialization
- How to Socialize Your Ragdoll
- Training Your Ragdoll
- Clicker Training Basics

- Scratching and Bad Behavior

CHAPTER 8
- ALL ABOUT THE LITTER BOX
  - Types of Litter Boxes
  - Litter Options
  - Litter Box Training
  - Common Problems
  - Toxoplasmosis

CHAPTER 9
- GROOMING YOUR RAGDOLL CAT
  - Brushing
  - Bathing
  - Trimming or Clipping
  - Nail Care
  - Ear and Eye Care
  - Finding a Groomer

CHAPTER 10
- FEEDING YOUR RAGDOLL
  - Benefits of Quality Nutrition
  - Commercial Diets
  - Homemade Diets
  - Ingredients to Avoid

CHAPTER 11
- YOUR RAGDOLL'S HEALTH CARE
  - Choosing a Vet
  - Microchipping
  - Vaccinations
  - Parasite Prevention

      Spaying and Neutering
      Declawing
      Common Genetic Conditions
      Pet Insurance

CHAPTER 12
   TRAVELING WITH YOUR RAGDOLL CAT
      Car Travel
      Air Travel
      Cat-Friendly Accommodations
      Leaving Your Cat Behind

CHAPTER 13
   INTO THE WORLD OF SHOWING
      All About Cat Shows
      Ragdoll Breed Standards
      Getting Started in Cat Shows

CHAPTER 14
   YOUR AGING RAGDOLL CAT
      Common Signs of Aging
      Basic Senior Cat Care
      Illness and Injury Prevention
      Senior Cat Nutrition

CHAPTER 15
   WHEN IT'S TIME TO SAY GOODBYE
      When to Say Goodbye
      The Euthanasia Process
      Final Arrangements
      Grieving Your Loss

CONCLUSION

**THE END**

## COPYRIGHT

Reservation of rights. Except for brief quotations used in critical reviews and certain other noncommercial uses allowed by copyright law, no part of this publication may be duplicated, distributed, or transmitted in any way without the publisher's prior written consent. This prohibition includes photocopying, recording, and other electronic or mechanical methods.

**Copyright © Steven white, 2024.**

# *Introduction*

Welcome to the world of Ragdoll cats, a breed that captivates the hearts of cat lovers everywhere with their stunning appearance and endearing personalities. This book is your comprehensive guide to understanding, caring for, and building a lifelong bond with one of the most beloved cat breeds in the world.

Ragdolls are known for their striking blue eyes, luxurious coats, and gentle, affectionate nature. But there is much more to these wonderful cats than meets the eye. Whether you're considering bringing a Ragdoll into your home, or you're already a proud Ragdoll owner, this book will provide you with all the information you need to ensure your feline friend thrives.

From the breed's fascinating history and unique characteristics to essential care tips and expert advice on health, grooming, and training, this guide covers every aspect of Ragdoll ownership. Whether you're preparing for the arrival of a kitten or navigating the later stages of your cat's life, you'll find practical advice and heartfelt insights to support you every step of the way.

Join us on this journey to discover why Ragdoll cats are truly a breed apart, offering

companionship, comfort, and love like no other.

# CHAPTER 1

## RAGDOLL CATS – A UNIQUE AND WONDERFUL BREED

### Physical Characteristics

Ragdoll cats are a strikingly beautiful and distinctive breed, easily recognizable by their large size, captivating blue eyes, and silky, semi-longhair coat. These cats are one of the largest domestic cat breeds, with males typically weighing between 15 to 20 pounds and females ranging from 10 to 15 pounds. Their broad chest, muscular build, and sturdy frame give them a powerful yet graceful appearance.

The coat of a Ragdoll is one of its most defining features. Unlike other long-haired breeds, Ragdolls have a silky texture that is surprisingly easy to maintain, as their fur does not tend to mat as easily. The coat comes in a variety of patterns and colors, with the most common being colorpoint, mitted, and bicolor. The color palette includes shades of seal, blue, chocolate, lilac, and even rarer hues like red and cream. This array of patterns and colors contributes to the Ragdoll's appeal, making each cat unique in its appearance.

Another notable physical characteristic of the Ragdoll is its eyes. Their large, oval-shaped eyes are typically a deep, vivid blue, which contrasts beautifully with their lighter fur, giving them an almost ethereal quality. This eye color is one of the breed's most enchanting features, drawing people in with their soulful, expressive gaze.

Ragdolls are also known for their distinctively soft, plush fur. Their coats are generally longer around the neck, forming a ruff or mane, and shorter on the face and legs. This luxurious fur, combined with their substantial size, makes them appear almost regal, a quality that is often highlighted in their calm and composed demeanor.

## *Temperament and Behavior*

Ragdoll cats are not just known for their physical beauty but also for their extraordinary temperament. They are often described as the "puppy-like" cats of the feline world due to their affectionate, gentle, and sociable nature. Unlike many cats that are independent and aloof, Ragdolls are known to follow their owners from room to room, seeking companionship and affection. They are extremely people-oriented and form strong bonds with their human families.

One of the most endearing traits of Ragdolls is their docile nature. They are famous for their tendency to go limp when picked up, a characteristic that earned them their name. This relaxed, floppy behavior is not just a physical response but also indicative of their trusting and laid-back personality. Ragdolls are generally quiet cats, with soft, gentle voices that they use sparingly, often preferring to communicate through their expressive eyes and body language.

Ragdolls are also known for their adaptability. They are typically calm in nature and do not easily get stressed by changes in their environment. This makes them well-suited for a variety of living situations, whether it's a busy household with children and other pets or a quiet, single-person home. Their even-tempered demeanor makes them excellent companions for families, as they are tolerant and patient, even with young children.

In terms of behavior, Ragdolls are known to be playful yet not overly energetic. They enjoy interactive play, such as chasing toys or engaging in games with their owners, but they are equally content lounging around the house. Their curiosity is balanced by a level-headed approach to new experiences, making them easy to train and manage.

## *Reaching Full Maturity*

Ragdoll cats are slow to mature, both physically and mentally. Unlike many other breeds that reach full maturity by the age of one or two, Ragdolls may not fully develop until they are about three to four years old. This extended development period is one of the reasons why they maintain a kitten-like playfulness well into adulthood.

Physically, Ragdolls continue to grow in size and muscle mass during this time. Their coat also goes through changes, often becoming fuller and more luxurious as they age. The colors and patterns of their coat may darken or become more defined over the years, adding to their already striking appearance.

Mentally, Ragdolls also mature at a slower pace. While they are intelligent and quick learners, their laid-back nature means they take their time to fully develop their personality traits. This slow maturation process allows them to remain playful and curious for longer, making them a delight to live with.

## *Is a Ragdoll Cat Right for You?*

Deciding whether a Ragdoll cat is the right fit for your home involves considering their unique characteristics and how they align with your lifestyle. Ragdolls thrive in environments where they can receive plenty of attention and affection. If you're looking for a cat that will be an integral part of your family, participating in daily activities and forming strong bonds with all members, a Ragdoll is an excellent choice.

However, it's important to consider their need for companionship. Ragdolls do not do well when left alone for long periods. If you work long hours or travel frequently, you might want to reconsider or ensure that your Ragdoll has a companion, whether it's another cat or a pet-friendly dog.

Their docile and gentle nature makes them ideal for households with children or other pets. They are generally tolerant and less likely to exhibit aggressive behavior, making them a safe choice for families. However, their relaxed nature also means they might not be the best fit for very active households where rough play is common.

In summary, if you're seeking a loyal, affectionate, and beautiful companion that will be a gentle presence in your home, a Ragdoll cat could be the perfect fit. Their unique combination of physical beauty and charming personality traits makes them a truly special breed, well-suited to those who can provide the love and attention they deserve.

# CHAPTER 2

## HISTORY OF THE RAGDOLL CAT

### The Origins of the Ragdoll

The Ragdoll cat, as we know it today, has a relatively recent history, tracing its origins back to the 1960s. This breed was developed by Ann Baker, a breeder in Riverside, California. Ann Baker's breeding program began with a domestic longhaired white cat named Josephine. Josephine is often regarded as the matriarch of the Ragdoll breed, though the full details of her lineage remain somewhat mysterious.

Josephine's kittens, according to Baker, displayed unique qualities that set them apart from other cats. They had a remarkably docile temperament, large size, and a tendency to go limp when picked up, which later became a defining trait of the Ragdoll breed. Intrigued by these characteristics, Baker began selectively breeding Josephine's offspring to establish a new breed that would consistently exhibit these traits.

Baker was meticulous in her breeding efforts, focusing on specific personality traits and physical attributes. She combined the genes from various long-haired cats, possibly including Burmese, Birman, and Persian breeds, though the exact breeds used have never been fully disclosed. Her goal was to create a cat that was not only aesthetically beautiful but also exceptionally gentle and affectionate.

One of the most interesting aspects of Baker's breeding program was her approach to establishing the Ragdoll as a breed. She was fiercely protective of her creation, going so far as to trademark the name "Ragdoll" and set strict guidelines for those interested in breeding them. This level of control was unusual in the cat breeding world and sparked both interest and controversy. However, it also helped maintain the breed's integrity and ensured that Ragdolls were bred to meet specific standards.

By the 1970s, Ragdoll cats had gained popularity, first in California and then across the United States. Despite initial skepticism from the broader cat breeding community, the breed's popularity continued to grow, eventually spreading to Europe and beyond. Today, Ragdolls are one of the most beloved cat breeds worldwide, known for their unique combination of size, beauty, and temperament.

## *Ragdoll Myths and Truths*

The history of the Ragdoll cat is also steeped in various myths and misconceptions, many of which originated from Ann Baker herself. One of the most persistent myths is that Ragdolls were the result of genetic manipulation or that they were bred to be immune to pain. Baker claimed that the docile nature of Ragdolls was due to a genetic mutation or experimental breeding, which made them unusually calm and less sensitive to pain. However, these claims have been widely discredited by veterinarians and geneticists. Ragdolls, like all cats, have a normal nervous system and are as sensitive to pain as any other breed.

Another myth surrounding Ragdolls is related to their tendency to go limp when held. Some have speculated that this behavior is a result of an abnormal nervous system or even a form of genetic defect. In reality, this characteristic is simply a reflection of the breed's exceptionally relaxed temperament and their trust in humans. When a Ragdoll goes limp in your arms, it is a sign of complete trust and comfort, not a neurological abnormality.

There are also myths regarding the breed's origin story. Some versions suggest that Josephine, the mother of all Ragdolls, was involved in a car accident, and her subsequent kittens were born with their unique temperament as a result of this trauma. While it's true that Josephine had a car accident, there is no scientific basis to support the idea that this incident led to the creation of the Ragdoll breed. Such stories are more folklore than fact, though they add an element of mystique to the breed's history.

Despite these myths, the truth about Ragdolls is equally fascinating. They were selectively bred to enhance specific traits calm demeanor, affectionate nature, and striking appearance without any need for genetic manipulation or extraordinary circumstances. The success of this selective breeding is evident in the Ragdoll's consistent temperament and physical characteristics, which have become the hallmark of the breed.

## *The Modern Ragdoll Cat*

Today's Ragdoll cats are the result of decades of careful breeding, with a focus on maintaining the qualities that Ann Baker originally sought to promote. The breed has been recognized by various cat fancier associations around the world, including The International Cat Association (TICA) and the Cat Fanciers' Association (CFA). These organizations have set standards for the breed, ensuring that Ragdolls bred today adhere to the physical and behavioral traits that have come to define them.

The modern Ragdoll cat is not only a beloved pet but also a show cat, competing in cat shows around the globe. These cats are judged based on specific criteria, including their size, coat quality, eye color, and overall temperament. The Ragdoll's success in these arenas has further cemented its reputation as a top-tier breed.

Ragdolls have also become popular as therapy animals, thanks to their calm and gentle nature. Their ability to bond closely with humans makes them ideal companions for those in need of emotional support. Whether it's visiting hospitals, schools, or nursing homes, Ragdolls often bring comfort and joy to those they encounter.

In the pet world, Ragdolls are highly sought after for their affectionate and easygoing nature. They are known to get along well with other pets, including dogs, and are particularly good with children. This makes them an ideal choice for families looking for a cat that is not only beautiful but also friendly and adaptable.

Despite their relatively recent history, Ragdoll cats have made a significant impact on the world of domestic cats. Their unique combination of size, beauty, and temperament has made them a favorite among cat lovers everywhere. As the breed continues to evolve, one thing remains certain: the Ragdoll cat, with its origins in California and its myths and truths, is a breed unlike any other.

# CHAPTER 3

## PURCHASING A RAGDOLL CAT

### Buying vs. Adopting

When considering adding a Ragdoll cat to your family, one of the first decisions you'll face is whether to buy from a breeder or adopt from a rescue or shelter. Each option has its advantages and challenges, and understanding them can help you make the best choice for your lifestyle and values.

#### Buying from a Breeder

Purchasing a Ragdoll cat from a reputable breeder can be a rewarding experience, especially if you are looking for a kitten with specific characteristics. Breeders who specialize in Ragdolls are often dedicated to maintaining the breed's standards, which means that the cats they produce typically exhibit the ideal physical traits and temperaments that make Ragdolls so beloved. When you buy from a breeder, you also have the opportunity to learn about the kitten's lineage, health history, and the environment in which it was raised.

A major advantage of buying from a breeder is the ability to start with a kitten. This allows you to be involved in the early stages of your cat's development, ensuring that it is well-socialized and integrated into your household from a young age. Additionally, many breeders offer health guarantees and are available for support and advice as your kitten grows.

However, buying from a breeder can be expensive. Ragdoll kittens from reputable breeders often come with a high price tag, reflecting the costs associated with responsible breeding practices. It's important to be aware that not all breeders are created equal. Some may prioritize profit over the well-being of their cats, leading to unethical practices such as overbreeding or inadequate care. It's crucial to do thorough research, visit the breeder's facility, and ask questions about their breeding practices before making a decision.

## *Adopting from a Rescue or Shelter*

Adopting a Ragdoll from a rescue or shelter can be a deeply fulfilling experience. Rescues and shelters often have cats that are in need of loving homes, and by adopting, you are giving a cat a second chance at a happy life. Adoption is also generally more affordable than buying from a breeder, with adoption fees typically covering vaccinations, spaying or neutering, and sometimes even microchipping.

One of the benefits of adopting is that you may find an adult Ragdoll who already has a well-established personality, making it easier to match the cat with your lifestyle. Adult cats from shelters are often already house-trained, and many have been exposed to a variety of environments, which can make the transition to a new home smoother.

That said, adopting from a shelter or rescue can come with its own set of challenges. Some cats in shelters may have unknown health or behavioral histories, which could require additional care and patience. It's also less likely that you will find a kitten at a shelter, so if you have your heart set on raising a Ragdoll from a very young age, adoption might not be the right choice for you.

Ultimately, the decision between buying and adopting should be based on your priorities, budget, and the type of experience you're seeking. Both options have the potential to bring a wonderful Ragdoll cat into your life; it's simply a matter of determining which path aligns best with your circumstances.

## *Rescues and Shelters*

If you decide that adoption is the route you want to take, finding a reputable rescue or shelter that specializes in Ragdolls or has them available can be a rewarding journey. Many rescues focus on specific breeds, including Ragdolls, and can be excellent resources for finding the perfect cat.

### _Ragdoll-Specific Rescues_

There are rescues dedicated exclusively to Ragdolls, and these organizations work tirelessly to rehome cats that have been surrendered, abandoned, or otherwise displaced. Ragdoll rescues are often run by individuals who are passionate about the breed and have extensive knowledge about their needs and personalities. These rescues often have rigorous adoption processes to ensure that the cats are placed in suitable, loving homes.

Ragdoll-specific rescues typically provide detailed information about the cats in their care, including health records, temperament assessments, and any special needs the cat might have. This level of information can be incredibly helpful in making an informed decision and ensuring a good match between the cat and your home.

### *Local Shelters*

Local animal shelters often have a variety of cats available for adoption, including purebred Ragdolls and Ragdoll mixes. While finding a Ragdoll at a general shelter might require more patience and persistence, it's not uncommon. Checking online databases, such as Petfinder or Adopt-a-Pet, can help you locate Ragdolls in shelters near you.

Adopting from a shelter can be a wonderful way to provide a home for a cat in need, and it often comes with the benefit of lower adoption fees. Shelters typically include vaccinations, spaying or neutering, and other basic care in the adoption fee, making it a cost-effective option.

### *Breed-Specific Rescue Networks*

In addition to individual rescues and shelters, there are networks of breed-specific rescue organizations that work together to find homes for Ragdolls across different regions. These networks can be invaluable in connecting you with available cats that match your criteria, even if they are located in a different state or country. Rescue networks often have transport options available to help get the cat to you, making it easier to adopt a Ragdoll even if one is not immediately available in your local area.

## *Tips for Adoption*

Adopting a Ragdoll cat, whether from a rescue or shelter, requires careful consideration and preparation to ensure a smooth transition for both you and the cat. Here are some tips to guide you through the adoption process:

**1. Research and Prepare:**
Before adopting, make sure you understand the specific needs of Ragdoll cats. This breed is known for its sociable and affectionate nature, so it's important to ensure that your lifestyle can accommodate a cat that craves interaction and companionship.

**2. Visit the Cat:**
If possible, visit the cat in person before

finalizing the adoption. This allows you to observe the cat's behavior, assess its temperament, and determine if it's a good fit for your home. Pay attention to how the cat reacts to you and other people, as well as how it behaves in the shelter or foster environment.

**3. Ask Questions:**
Don't hesitate to ask the rescue or shelter staff about the cat's history, health, and personality. The more you know, the better prepared you'll be to meet the cat's needs. Inquire about any known behavioral issues, dietary preferences, or medical conditions that might require special attention.

**4. Prepare Your Home:**
Before bringing your new Ragdoll home, ensure that your living space is ready. Set up a comfortable area with all the necessary supplies, including food, water, a litter box, and toys. Ragdolls thrive in environments where they feel secure, so consider creating a quiet space where your new cat can retreat if it feels overwhelmed.

### 5. Be Patient:

Adjusting to a new home can be stressful for any cat, especially one that has been in a shelter or rescue environment. Give your Ragdoll time to acclimate to its new surroundings and be patient as it settles in. Providing consistent love and attention will help your cat feel secure and comfortable in its new home.

By following these tips and considering all your options carefully, you can find a wonderful Ragdoll cat to join your family, bringing joy and companionship for years to come.

# *CHAPTER 4*

## *ALL ABOUT RAGDOLL BREEDERS*

### *Finding a Reputable Breeder*

Finding a reputable Ragdoll breeder is a crucial step in acquiring a healthy and well-socialized kitten. A good breeder not only ensures that you receive a cat with excellent physical and behavioral traits but also provides a foundation for a positive and supportive relationship as you raise your new pet.

#### *Research and Referrals*

Start by researching breeders in your area or within a reasonable distance. Online directories, breed clubs, and forums can be valuable resources. Reputable breeders often have affiliations with recognized breed clubs, such as

The International Cat Association (TICA) or the Cat Fanciers' Association (CFA). These affiliations can be a sign of a breeder's commitment to maintaining breed standards. Referrals from trusted sources, such as veterinarians or Ragdoll cat owners, can also be helpful. Personal recommendations provide insights into the breeder's reputation and the experiences of others who have purchased cats from them.

### *Visit the Breeder*
Once you've identified potential breeders, arrange visits to their facilities. A visit allows you to assess the conditions in which the cats are raised. The environment should be clean, well-maintained, and conducive to the health and well-being of the cats. Pay attention to the overall health and demeanor of the cats and kittens. They should be active, alert, and well-socialized.

During your visit, ask to see the breeding cats and their living conditions. A reputable breeder will be open to showing you their facilities and answering questions about their breeding practices. This transparency is a good indicator of the breeder's commitment to ethical practices and the welfare of their cats.

### *Questions to Ask*
Prepare a list of questions to ask the breeder. Inquire about their breeding practices, including the health and genetic background of the parent cats. Ask about the frequency of breeding and the age at which the cats are retired from breeding. A responsible breeder will limit the number of litters and ensure that the cats are given adequate time to rest between litters.

### *References and Reviews*
Ask the breeder for references from previous kitten buyers. Speaking with other families who have purchased kittens from the breeder can provide valuable insights into their experiences. Online reviews and testimonials can also help gauge the breeder's reputation and the quality of their cats.

## *Health Tests and Certifications*

Ensuring that your Ragdoll kitten is healthy is a top priority, and reputable breeders will conduct a range of health tests and provide certifications to support the well-being of their cats.

### *Genetic Testing*

A responsible Ragdoll breeder will perform genetic testing on their breeding cats to screen for common hereditary conditions. These tests help identify genetic disorders that could be passed on to the kittens. Common tests for Ragdolls include those for hypertrophic cardiomyopathy (HCM), a heart condition, and other breed-specific genetic issues. The breeder should be able to provide documentation of these tests and their results.

### *Health Clearances*

In addition to genetic testing, breeding cats should receive regular health clearances from a veterinarian. These clearances typically include examinations for common health issues such as feline leukemia (FeLV) and feline immunodeficiency virus (FIV). The breeder should provide certificates or documentation showing that their cats have been tested and cleared of these diseases.

## *Vaccinations and Preventive Care*

Kittens should receive their initial vaccinations and preventive care before they leave the breeder's home. This includes vaccinations against common diseases such as feline distemper and upper respiratory infections. The breeder should provide a vaccination record and any other relevant health documentation for your kitten.

## *Health Guarantees*

Reputable breeders often provide health guarantees as part of their contract. This guarantee typically covers specific health conditions and may offer a replacement kitten or reimbursement if a serious health issue is discovered within a certain timeframe. Review the health guarantee carefully to understand what is covered and any requirements for reporting health issues.

## Breeder Contracts and Guarantees

A breeder contract is an important document that outlines the terms of the sale and the responsibilities of both the breeder and the buyer. It helps ensure a clear understanding of the terms and conditions of the purchase and protects both parties.

Key Components of a Breeder Contract:
A typical breeder contract will include details about the kitten's health, any warranties or guarantees provided, and the breeder's responsibilities. It may also outline the buyer's responsibilities, such as providing proper care and not breeding the kitten without the breeder's consent. Ensure that the contract specifies what happens if a serious health issue arises and how disputes will be resolved.

### *Health Guarantees*

The health guarantee section of the contract should clearly state the duration of coverage and the conditions that are covered. It may include provisions for replacement or reimbursement if the kitten is diagnosed with a genetic disorder or other serious health issue within a specified period. Review this section carefully and ask the breeder to clarify any terms you do not understand.

## *Spay/Neuter Agreements*
Many breeders require that kittens be spayed or neutered by a certain age. This agreement helps prevent unwanted litters and ensures that the kitten is not used for breeding purposes without proper planning. The contract should specify when the spay/neuter procedure should be completed and any associated requirements.

## **Return Policies**
The contract may include a return policy that outlines the conditions under which the kitten can be returned to the breeder. This policy is typically in place to ensure that the kitten has a safe and supportive environment if the new owner is unable to keep it. Understand the terms of the return policy and any associated fees or conditions.

## Choosing Your Perfect Kitten

Choosing the right Ragdoll kitten involves more than just selecting a cat with the right appearance. It's essential to consider personality, health, and how well the kitten will fit into your home.

### *Assessing Personality*
Spend time interacting with the kittens to assess their personalities. Look for signs of sociability, curiosity, and comfort around people. Ragdoll kittens are typically affectionate and enjoy being held, but individual personalities can vary. Consider how a kitten's temperament aligns with your lifestyle and preferences.

### *Health and Development*
Examine the kitten's overall health and development. Healthy kittens should be active, alert, and have clear eyes and a clean coat. Check for any signs of illness or discomfort, such as coughing, sneezing, or diarrhea. Discuss the kitten's health history with the breeder and review any health records provided.

### _Compatibility with Your Home_

Consider how the kitten will fit into your household. If you have other pets or young children, choose a kitten that seems adaptable and comfortable in a multi-pet environment. A well-socialized kitten should adjust smoothly to new situations and people.

### _Trust Your Instincts_

Ultimately, trust your instincts when choosing a kitten. You should feel a connection with the kitten and a sense of confidence in its health and well-being. Take your time to make an informed decision and ensure that you are ready to provide a loving and supportive home for your new Ragdoll.

## Adopting Multiple Cats

If you are considering adopting more than one Ragdoll cat, there are several factors to keep in mind to ensure a smooth transition and a harmonious household.

## *Benefits of Multiple Cats*

Adopting multiple Ragdolls can provide companionship and enrichment for each cat. Cats are social animals, and having a playmate can help alleviate boredom and reduce stress. Ragdolls, in particular, are known for their sociable and gentle nature, which can make them well-suited to living with other cats.

## *Introducing New Cats*

Proper introductions are crucial when bringing multiple cats into your home. Start by keeping the new cats separated in different rooms with their own food, water, and litter boxes. Gradually introduce them to each other through scent and supervised interactions. Monitor their behavior closely and provide plenty of positive reinforcement to encourage positive interactions.

## *Space and Resources*

Ensure that your home has enough space and resources for multiple cats. Provide multiple litter boxes, scratching posts, and resting areas to prevent territorial disputes and ensure that each cat has its own space. Adequate resources and space can help reduce competition and promote a harmonious environment.

### *Monitoring Health*
When adopting multiple cats, be vigilant about their health and well-being. Regular veterinary check-ups, vaccinations, and preventive care are essential to keep all your cats healthy. Watch for any signs of illness or behavioral issues and address them promptly.

By following these guidelines and considering the needs of both individual cats and the group as a whole, you can create a happy and balanced environment for your Ragdoll family. Whether you choose to adopt a single kitten or multiple cats, providing love, care, and attention will ensure that your Ragdolls thrive and become cherished members of your home.

# CHAPTER 5

## PREPARING FOR YOUR RAGDOLL CAT

### Necessary Supplies

Bringing a Ragdoll cat into your home requires careful preparation to ensure that you have all the necessary supplies for a smooth transition. Ragdolls, known for their gentle and affectionate nature, need a comfortable and well-equipped environment to thrive.

#### *Basic Supplies*
Start with the essentials: a litter box, food and water bowls, and a scratching post. The litter box should be large enough for your Ragdoll to use comfortably, with low sides for easy access.

Choose a high-quality litter that controls odor and is gentle on your cat's paws.

Food and water bowls should be sturdy and easy to clean. Consider using ceramic or stainless steel bowls, as they are less likely to harbor bacteria compared to plastic. Ensure that the bowls are appropriately sized for your cat and are placed in a quiet, accessible area.

A scratching post or cat tree is crucial for your Ragdoll's physical and mental well-being. Ragdolls, like all cats, have a natural instinct to scratch. Providing a scratching post helps keep their claws healthy and prevents damage to your furniture. Choose a scratching post with different textures and heights to accommodate your cat's preferences.

### *Comfort and Enrichment*
Invest in a comfortable bed or cat condo where your Ragdoll can sleep and relax. Ragdolls enjoy cozy, enclosed spaces, so providing a soft, cushioned area will make them feel secure and

comfortable. Look for beds that are machine washable for easy maintenance.

Toys and enrichment items are also important for keeping your Ragdoll mentally stimulated and entertained. Interactive toys, such as feather wands or laser pointers, can provide exercise and engagement. Catnip toys can also be a fun addition, though not all cats respond to catnip.

## *Grooming Supplies*

Ragdolls have semi-long fur that requires regular grooming to prevent matting and tangles. Invest in a high-quality cat brush or comb to keep your Ragdoll's coat in good condition. Additionally, have nail clippers and a grooming mat on hand for regular maintenance.

## *Health Essentials*

Make sure you have the basics for health care, including a carrier for trips to the veterinarian and any medications or supplements your Ragdoll may need. A well-ventilated carrier will make trips to the vet more comfortable and stress-free.

## *Preparing Your Other Pets*

If you have other pets, it's important to prepare them for the arrival of your new Ragdoll cat to ensure a smooth introduction and harmonious coexistence.

### *Gradual Introductions*
Introduce your new Ragdoll to your existing pets gradually. Begin by allowing your other pets to become familiar with the scent of the new cat. You can do this by placing a blanket or bedding from the new cat in areas where your other pets spend time. This helps them get used to the new scent without direct contact.

When the time comes for a face-to-face introduction, ensure that the meeting takes place in a neutral space. Avoid introducing the new Ragdoll to your existing pets in a territory that is already claimed by the current pets, as this can lead to territorial disputes.

### _Supervised Meetings_

During initial introductions, supervise all interactions closely. Keep the Ragdoll in a separate room with its own food, water, and litter box until everyone is comfortable with each other. Allow the pets to sniff each other under the door or through a baby gate before letting them meet directly.

### _Positive Reinforcement_

Encourage positive interactions by rewarding all pets with treats and praise for calm behavior. Avoid punishing pets for any aggressive or fearful reactions, as this can exacerbate anxiety and aggression. Instead, redirect their attention with toys or treats to create positive associations with the new Ragdoll.

### _Monitoring Behavior_

Pay close attention to the behavior of all pets during the transition period. Look for signs of stress or aggression and address them promptly. It may take time for everyone to adjust, so be patient and provide support as needed.

## Preparing Your Children and Family

Preparing your family, especially children, for the arrival of a new Ragdoll cat is essential to ensure a smooth integration into your home.

### *Education and Expectations*
Teach your children about how to interact with the new cat gently and respectfully. Explain that Ragdolls, like all cats, need their space and may not always want to be held or petted. Emphasize the importance of handling the cat gently and avoiding sudden movements or loud noises that might startle it.

### *Setting Rules*
Establish clear rules for interacting with the cat, such as not picking it up without permission or not bothering it while it is eating or sleeping. Make sure the rules are age-appropriate and easy for your children to understand and follow.

### *Involvement in Care*
Involve your children in the care of the new cat, such as feeding, grooming, or playing with it.

This can help them develop a sense of responsibility and a bond with the cat. Supervise their interactions to ensure that they are gentle and appropriate.

### *Creating Safe Spaces*

Ensure that your Ragdoll has a safe space where it can retreat if it feels overwhelmed. This space should be off-limits to children and other pets, providing the cat with a quiet, secure area where it can relax and feel safe.

## Kitten-Proofing Your Home

Kitten-proofing your home is crucial to ensure the safety of your new Ragdoll and prevent any accidents or damage.

### *Secure Hazardous Items*

Remove or secure any hazardous items that your Ragdoll might chew on or play with. This includes electrical cords, small objects, and toxic plants. Consider using cord protectors to prevent chewing on wires and removing small items that could be swallowed.

Protecting Furniture and Valuables

Protect your furniture and valuables by providing alternative scratching posts and play areas for your Ragdoll. Cover or move items that might be easily knocked over or damaged. If you have breakable items, consider placing them out of reach or in cabinets with secure closures.

### **_Safe Spaces_**

Create safe spaces where your Ragdoll can play and explore without encountering hazards. Ensure that any areas where the cat has access are free from small objects, chemicals, or anything that could pose a risk to its health and safety.

### **_Litter Box Location_**

Place the litter box in a quiet, accessible area where your Ragdoll can use it without feeling threatened or exposed. Avoid placing the litter box near the cat's food and water bowls, as this can lead to reluctance to use it.

## *The First Few Weeks*

The first few weeks after bringing your Ragdoll cat home are crucial for establishing a positive relationship and helping the cat adjust to its new environment.

### *Establishing Routine*
Establish a consistent routine for feeding, grooming, and playtime. Ragdolls thrive on routine, and a consistent schedule helps them feel secure and settled. Stick to regular feeding times and provide a predictable environment to reduce stress.

### *Gradual Exploration*
Allow your Ragdoll to explore its new home gradually. Start by confining it to one room and gradually introduce it to other areas of the house as it becomes more comfortable. Monitor its behavior and provide reassurance as needed.

### *Bonding Time*
Spend quality time bonding with your Ragdoll through gentle play and affectionate interactions.

This helps build trust and strengthens your relationship. Use interactive toys and engage in gentle play to help your cat feel comfortable and secure.

### *Monitoring Health*
Monitor your Ragdoll's health and behavior closely during the first few weeks. Keep an eye out for any signs of illness or discomfort and contact your veterinarian if you have any concerns. Regular check-ups and vaccinations should be scheduled as recommended by your vet.

### *Creating a Positive Experience*
Ensure that the transition to your home is a positive experience for your Ragdoll. Provide plenty of positive reinforcement, such as treats and praise, for calm and confident behavior. Avoid overwhelming your cat with too many new experiences at once, and allow it to acclimate at its own pace.

By preparing thoroughly and providing a supportive environment, you can help your

Ragdoll cat settle into its new home comfortably and enjoy a happy, healthy life with you.

# CHAPTER 6

## CARING FOR YOUR RAGDOLL CAT

### Indoor or Outdoor

When it comes to deciding whether your Ragdoll cat should be an indoor or outdoor pet, there are several factors to consider. Ragdolls are known for their gentle and laid-back personalities, which often make them better suited for indoor living. Their placid nature, combined with their semi-long fur, can pose specific challenges in an outdoor environment.

***Indoor Living***
Indoor living offers numerous advantages for Ragdolls. One of the primary benefits is safety. Indoor cats are protected from hazards such as traffic, predators, diseases, and harsh weather

conditions. Ragdolls, due to their friendly and trusting nature, may not have the instinctual street smarts needed to navigate outdoor dangers.

Moreover, indoor living allows for better control over your Ragdoll's diet and health care. You can monitor their food intake, provide a controlled environment for exercise, and ensure regular veterinary check-ups without the risks associated with outdoor roaming.

### *Outdoor Access*
If you are considering giving your Ragdoll outdoor access, it's crucial to take several precautions. Some owners opt for enclosed outdoor spaces, such as catios or secure backyard areas, to provide a safe environment where their cats can enjoy the outdoors without the risks associated with free-roaming.

Outdoor access can offer mental stimulation and physical exercise, but it also requires diligent supervision and planning. Ensure that your outdoor space is escape-proof and free from hazards. Additionally, consider the climate and environmental conditions to ensure that your Ragdoll is comfortable and safe.

## *Emotional Needs*

Ragdolls are known for their affectionate and sociable nature. Meeting their emotional needs is essential for their overall well-being and happiness. These cats thrive on companionship and interaction, making them particularly responsive to their human families.

### *Affection and Attention*
Ragdolls are often described as "puppy-like" in their desire for human interaction. They enjoy being held, cuddled, and included in family activities. Regular, affectionate interactions help strengthen the bond between you and your Ragdoll. Spend time petting, talking to, and playing with your cat to fulfill its need for emotional connection.

### *Socialization*
Early socialization is crucial for Ragdolls.

Kittens that are well-socialized with a variety of people, animals, and experiences tend to grow up to be more confident and adaptable. Continue to provide positive social experiences throughout their lives to keep them well-adjusted and happy.

### *Responding to Behavior*

Pay attention to your Ragdoll's behavior to understand its emotional needs. Signs of stress or anxiety, such as hiding, excessive grooming, or changes in appetite, may indicate that your cat needs more attention or a change in its environment. Address any issues promptly and provide reassurance and comfort.

### *A Safe Retreat*

Providing a safe retreat for your Ragdoll is essential for its sense of security and well-being. A safe retreat offers a quiet, comfortable space where your cat can relax and escape from any stressors or disturbances.

### *Designated Safe Space*

Create a designated area in your home where

your Ragdoll can retreat when it needs to. This space should be quiet, cozy, and away from the hustle and bustle of daily activities. A soft bed or cat condo in a secluded corner can serve as a perfect retreat.

### *Comfort and Security*
Ensure that the safe retreat area is equipped with all the essentials your Ragdoll needs, such as food, water, and a litter box if the space is large enough. Adding familiar items, such as your cat's favorite blanket or toys, can help make the area feel more secure and comforting.

### *Respecting Privacy*
Respect your Ragdoll's need for privacy and alone time. If your cat retreats to its safe space, allow it to stay there undisturbed. Forcing interaction or intruding on its retreat can increase stress and anxiety.

## *Hairballs*

Hairballs are a common issue for Ragdolls due to their semi-long fur. Regular grooming and care can help minimize the occurrence of hairballs and keep your cat's coat healthy and tangle-free.

### *Grooming*
Regular grooming is essential for Ragdolls to prevent hairballs. Brush your cat's fur several times a week to remove loose hair and prevent mats and tangles. Use a high-quality cat brush or comb designed for long-haired breeds to effectively manage your Ragdoll's coat.

### *Diet and Supplements*
A well-balanced diet can also help reduce hairballs. Consider feeding your Ragdoll a high-quality cat food that supports healthy skin and coat. Some specialized cat foods contain added fiber to help with hairball control. Additionally, hairball control treats or supplements can be beneficial. Consult your veterinarian for recommendations on the best dietary options and supplements for your Ragdoll.

### *Monitoring Health*

Keep an eye on your Ragdoll's grooming habits and overall health. If you notice signs of excessive hairballs, such as coughing, gagging, or vomiting, consult your veterinarian. Frequent hairball issues may require additional interventions or changes in diet and grooming routines.

## *Enrichment and Playtime*

Providing enrichment and playtime is crucial for keeping your Ragdoll mentally stimulated and physically active. Enrichment activities help prevent boredom and promote a happy, healthy lifestyle.

### *Interactive Toys*

Invest in a variety of interactive toys to engage your Ragdoll's natural hunting instincts. Toys such as feather wands, laser pointers, and puzzle toys can provide both physical exercise and mental stimulation. Rotate toys regularly to keep your cat's interest and prevent boredom.

### *Playtime Routine*

Establish a regular playtime routine with your Ragdoll. Engage in interactive play sessions several times a day to keep your cat active and entertained. Playtime helps strengthen the bond between you and your cat and provides an outlet for energy and curiosity.

### *Environmental Enrichment*

Create an enriching environment by providing climbing structures, scratching posts, and window perches. Ragdolls enjoy observing their surroundings from elevated spots and appreciate opportunities to climb and explore. Enriching your cat's environment helps satisfy its natural instincts and provides a stimulating space to enjoy.

### *Social Interaction*

Ragdolls thrive on social interaction, so spend quality time with your cat. Include it in family activities and provide opportunities for social engagement. A well-socialized Ragdoll enjoys being part of the family and benefits from regular interaction and companionship.

By addressing these aspects of care, you can ensure that your Ragdoll cat remains healthy, happy, and well-adjusted. Providing a safe, enriched environment and meeting your cat's emotional and physical needs will contribute to a fulfilling and rewarding relationship with your furry companion.

# CHAPTER 7

## TRAINING AND SOCIALIZATION

### The Importance of Socialization

Socialization is a critical aspect of raising a well-adjusted Ragdoll cat. It involves exposing your kitten to a variety of people, environments, and experiences to ensure that it grows up to be a confident, adaptable, and friendly adult cat. For Ragdolls, who are known for their gentle and sociable nature, early and ongoing socialization is especially important to nurture their inherent affectionate traits.

***Building Confidence***
Early socialization helps build a kitten's confidence and reduces the likelihood of developing behavioral issues later in life. Kittens that are exposed to different stimuli in a positive, controlled manner learn to handle new situations

with ease. This early exposure helps them become more adaptable to changes and less likely to react fearfully to unfamiliar people, animals, or environments.

### *Positive Interactions*
Socialization also teaches kittens how to interact positively with people and other pets. Ragdolls, in particular, thrive on social interaction and enjoy being part of family activities. By introducing them to various experiences and ensuring these encounters are positive, you help them develop a friendly and trusting nature.

### *Preventing Behavioral Issues*
A well-socialized Ragdoll is less likely to exhibit aggressive or fearful behavior. Socialization helps prevent issues such as hiding, excessive aggression, or anxiety around strangers. Cats that have been properly socialized are generally more comfortable in new environments and more accepting of changes in their routine.

## *How to Socialize Your Ragdoll*

Socializing your Ragdoll involves a combination of gradual exposure to new experiences and positive reinforcement. Here's a step-by-step guide to effectively socialize your kitten:

### *Start Early*

Begin socializing your Ragdoll kitten as early as possible. The critical socialization period for kittens is between 2 and 9 weeks of age. During this time, they are most receptive to new experiences and can adapt quickly to new stimuli.

### *Introduce New Experiences Gradually*

Introduce your Ragdoll to new experiences and stimuli gradually. Start with less intimidating situations, such as gently introducing new toys or playing soothing sounds. Gradually increase the complexity of the experiences, such as introducing new people or other pets, ensuring that each introduction is positive and not overwhelming.

### *Positive Reinforcement*

Use positive reinforcement to create positive

associations with new experiences. Reward your Ragdoll with treats, praise, and affection whenever it exhibits calm and confident behavior in response to new stimuli. This approach helps reinforce positive responses and encourages your kitten to approach new situations with curiosity rather than fear.

### *Socialize with Different People*
Expose your Ragdoll to a variety of people, including men, women, and children, to ensure it becomes comfortable around individuals of all ages and appearances. Encourage visitors to interact with your kitten gently and positively, allowing it to become accustomed to different voices, smells, and appearances.

### *Interaction with Other Pets*
If you have other pets, introduce them to your Ragdoll in a controlled and gradual manner. Allow your kitten to observe the other pets from a safe distance before any direct interactions. Monitor their behavior closely and provide positive reinforcement for calm and friendly interactions.

### *Handling and Grooming*

Get your Ragdoll used to being handled and groomed early on. Gently hold and stroke your kitten, and introduce it to grooming tools, such as brushes and nail clippers. Positive reinforcement during these activities helps your Ragdoll associate handling and grooming with positive experiences.

## *Training Your Ragdoll*

Training is an important aspect of raising a well-behaved Ragdoll cat. Training helps establish boundaries, encourages positive behavior, and enhances the bond between you and your cat. While Ragdolls are generally cooperative and eager to please, consistent training methods are essential for achieving desired results.

### *Basic Commands*

Start with basic commands, such as "sit," "come," or "stay." Use a combination of verbal cues and hand signals to teach these commands. Begin with short training sessions and keep them positive and engaging. Reward your Ragdoll with treats and praise for correctly following commands.

### *Clicker Training*
Clicker training is a highly effective method for training Ragdolls. It involves using a clicker to mark the exact moment your cat performs a desired behavior, followed by a reward. The clicker's sound serves as a clear, consistent signal that the behavior was correct, helping your Ragdoll understand what is expected.

### *Consistency and Patience*
Consistency is key in training. Use the same commands and cues consistently to avoid confusing your Ragdoll. Training sessions should be short, positive, and frequent. Patience is essential, as it may take time for your Ragdoll to learn new commands and behaviors.

### *Addressing Behavioral Issues*
If your Ragdoll exhibits undesirable behaviors, address them promptly and calmly. Avoid

punishment, as it can create fear and stress. Instead, redirect your cat's attention to more appropriate behaviors and reward positive actions.

## *Clicker Training Basics*

Clicker training is a popular and effective training method for Ragdolls due to its clear and positive reinforcement approach. The clicker is a small device that makes a distinct clicking sound when pressed. This sound is used to mark the exact moment your Ragdoll performs a desired behavior, making it easier for the cat to understand what is being rewarded.

### *Introducing the Clicker*
Start by introducing your Ragdoll to the clicker. Click the device and immediately reward your cat with a treat. Repeat this several times to help your Ragdoll associate the clicking sound with receiving a reward. This process is known as "charging the clicker" and helps your cat understand that the clicker's sound means a reward is coming.

### *Teaching Basic Commands*
Once your Ragdoll is familiar with the clicker, begin teaching basic commands or tricks. Use a simple command, such as "sit," and prompt your cat to perform the behavior. Click and reward immediately when your Ragdoll follows the command. Repeat the process consistently until your cat reliably performs the command in response to the cue.

### *Gradual Progression*
As your Ragdoll learns basic commands, you can gradually introduce more complex behaviors or tricks. Use the clicker to mark each successful step toward the desired behavior and provide rewards accordingly. Break down complex behaviors into smaller steps to make the learning process manageable for your cat.

### *Maintaining Engagement*
Keep training sessions short and engaging to maintain your Ragdoll's interest. Aim for several short sessions each day rather than one long

session. Always end training on a positive note with a successful behavior and reward, reinforcing your cat's enthusiasm for learning.

## Scratching and Bad Behavior

Scratching is a natural behavior for cats, including Ragdolls. It helps them maintain healthy claws and mark their territory. However, scratching can sometimes lead to unwanted behavior if not managed properly.

### *Providing Scratching Outlets*
To prevent your Ragdoll from scratching furniture or other undesirable areas, provide appropriate scratching posts or pads. Place these scratching surfaces in locations where your cat frequently scratches, such as near its sleeping area or where it previously scratched furniture.

### *Encouraging Use*
Encourage your Ragdoll to use the scratching posts by rubbing them with catnip or placing treats near them. You can also use toys to attract your cat to the scratching post. Positive

reinforcement, such as praise and treats, can help your Ragdoll associate the scratching post with positive experiences.

## *Addressing Destructive Scratching*

If your Ragdoll continues to scratch furniture or other undesired areas, use deterrents to discourage the behavior. Cover the furniture with double-sided tape or use commercial deterrent sprays. Ensure that the scratching posts are attractive and accessible to reduce the likelihood of your cat resorting to unwanted scratching.

## *Training for Bad Behavior*

For other behavioral issues, such as jumping on counters or excessive meowing, use positive reinforcement to encourage alternative behaviors. Redirect your Ragdoll's attention to a more appropriate activity and reward it for engaging in the desired behavior. Consistent training and patience are key to modifying unwanted behaviors.

By focusing on effective socialization and training techniques, you can help your Ragdoll develop into a well-behaved and confident adult cat. Providing positive reinforcement, consistent training, and addressing behavioral issues promptly will enhance your relationship with your Ragdoll and ensure a happy, harmonious home environment.

# CHAPTER 8

## ALL ABOUT THE LITTER BOX

### Types of Litter Boxes

Selecting the right litter box is an important aspect of ensuring your Ragdoll cat's comfort and maintaining a clean, hygienic environment. There are several types of litter boxes to choose from, each with its own benefits and considerations.

**<u>Open Litter Boxes</u>**
Open litter boxes are the most common type and consist of a simple, uncovered box. They are easy to clean and allow for easy access, which is beneficial for cats that are still adjusting to using a litter box. Open boxes are also typically less expensive and come in various sizes to accommodate different needs.

### Covered Litter Boxes

Covered litter boxes have a lid or cover that helps contain odors and reduce the spread of litter outside the box. The cover often includes a door or flap for your Ragdoll to enter and exit. While covered boxes can help keep the surrounding area cleaner, some cats may find them less inviting or more difficult to use. Ensure that the cover is removable or easily cleaned to prevent odor build-up.

### Self-Cleaning Litter Boxes

Self-cleaning litter boxes use automatic mechanisms to scoop waste and clean the litter. These boxes are convenient for busy pet owners and can help maintain a cleaner environment with minimal effort. However, they can be more expensive and require regular maintenance and battery or power source.

### Top-Entry Litter Boxes

Top-entry litter boxes feature an opening on the top of the box, which requires your Ragdoll to jump or climb into the box. These are effective at preventing litter from being scattered outside the box, but some cats may find the top-entry design challenging to use, particularly older or less agile cats.

### *High-Sided Litter Boxes*
High-sided litter boxes have elevated sides that help contain litter and prevent it from being kicked out of the box. These boxes are useful for cats that tend to dig or scratch excessively. Ensure the box is not too tall for your Ragdoll to comfortably enter and exit.

## *Litter Options*

Choosing the right type of litter is crucial for both your Ragdoll's comfort and the cleanliness of your home. There are various litter options available, each with its own advantages and drawbacks.

### *Clumping Clay Litter*
Clumping clay litter is one of the most popular types and forms clumps when it comes into contact with moisture. This makes it easy to

scoop out waste and keep the litter box clean. It is available in both clumping and non-clumping varieties. Clumping litter often uses sodium bentonite clay, which is absorbent and controls odors effectively.

### *Non-Clumping Clay Litter*
Non-clumping clay litter absorbs moisture but does not form clumps. This type of litter requires more frequent changes to maintain cleanliness and control odors. Non-clumping litter can be less efficient at odor control compared to clumping varieties, but it can be a good option for cats with sensitive paws.

### *Biodegradable Litter*
Biodegradable litters are made from natural materials such as corn, wheat, wood, or paper. These litters are environmentally friendly and often more gentle on your cat's paws. They can be clumping or non-clumping and generally offer good odor control. Biodegradable litters may need to be changed more frequently compared to clay litters.

### *Silica Gel Litter*

Silica gel litter is made from tiny silica crystals that absorb moisture and control odors. It is low-dust and typically requires less frequent changes. However, some cats may find the texture of silica gel litter less appealing, and it can be more expensive compared to other types.

### *Crystal Litter*

Crystal litter is similar to silica gel and is designed to absorb moisture and control odors effectively. It is low-dust and non-clumping, making it easy to clean. Crystal litter often needs to be replaced entirely when it becomes saturated, rather than scooping out waste.

## Litter Box Training

Training your Ragdoll to use the litter box is essential for maintaining a clean home and ensuring your cat's comfort. Most kittens learn to use the litter box instinctively, but some may require additional guidance.

### *Initial Placement*

Place the litter box in a quiet, accessible location where your Ragdoll can easily find it. Avoid placing the box near the cat's food and water bowls, as cats prefer to keep their eating and elimination areas separate. A quiet, private corner is ideal for a litter box.

### *Encouraging Use*

If your Ragdoll is a kitten or new to your home, gently place it in the litter box after meals, naps, and playtime to encourage use. Most cats will naturally start using the box after being placed in it a few times. You can also gently scratch the litter with your hand to show your cat how to dig and cover its waste.

### *Maintaining Cleanliness*

Keep the litter box clean by scooping it daily and changing the litter regularly. Cats are sensitive to cleanliness, and a dirty litter box can lead to reluctance to use it. Wash the litter box with mild soap and water during litter changes to prevent odors and bacteria build-up.

### *Positive Reinforcement*

Reward your Ragdoll with treats and praise for using the litter box correctly. Positive reinforcement helps your cat associate the litter box with a rewarding experience, reinforcing the behavior.

### *Handling Accidents*

If your Ragdoll has an accident outside the litter box, clean the area thoroughly with an enzymatic cleaner to remove odors. Avoid punishing your cat, as this can create fear and anxiety. Instead, review the litter box placement and cleanliness and ensure that the box is easily accessible.

## Common Problems

While most Ragdolls adapt well to using a litter box, there are some common problems that can arise. Addressing these issues promptly can help maintain a clean and stress-free environment for your cat.

### *Inappropriate Elimination*

If your Ragdoll is eliminated outside the litter box, it could be due to a variety of reasons, including stress, medical issues, or dissatisfaction with the litter box setup. Evaluate factors such as the box's location, cleanliness, and litter type. Consult your veterinarian if the issue persists, as it may be a sign of a urinary tract infection or other health concerns.

### *Litter Box Aversion*

Litter box aversion can occur if your Ragdoll associates the box with negative experiences, such as pain or discomfort. Ensure the litter box is clean, the litter is comfortable, and there are no signs of injury or illness. Gradually reintroduce the box in a positive, stress-free manner.

### *Litter Tracking*

Litter tracking, where litter is spread outside the box, can be minimized by using a litter mat or placing a rug under the box. High-sided boxes and those with covers can also help reduce litter scatter. Regular cleaning of the surrounding area is important to maintain hygiene.

## *Toxoplasmosis*

Toxoplasmosis is a parasitic infection caused by Toxoplasma gondii, which can affect both cats and humans. Understanding the risks and prevention strategies is important for ensuring the health of both your Ragdoll and your household.

### *Transmission*
Cats can become infected with Toxoplasma gondii by ingesting contaminated food, water, or prey. The parasite is shed in the cat's feces and can contaminate the environment. Humans can contract toxoplasmosis through contact with contaminated soil, cat feces, or undercooked meat.

### *Symptoms*
In cats, toxoplasmosis may cause symptoms such as diarrhea, vomiting, lethargy, and loss of appetite. Some cats may not show any symptoms

but can still shed the parasite. If you notice any of these symptoms in your Ragdoll, consult your veterinarian for diagnosis and treatment.

### ***Prevention***
To reduce the risk of toxoplasmosis, practice good hygiene by regularly cleaning the litter box and washing your hands thoroughly after handling cat litter. Avoid handling soiled litter with bare hands and consider using gloves when cleaning the box. Keep your Ragdoll indoors to reduce exposure to potential sources of infection.

### ***Veterinary Care***
Regular veterinary check-ups are essential for monitoring your Ragdoll's health and preventing parasitic infections. Discuss any concerns or symptoms with your veterinarian, who can provide guidance on preventing and treating toxoplasmosis and other health issues.

By understanding and addressing these aspects of litter box care, you can ensure that your Ragdoll remains comfortable, healthy, and well-adjusted. A clean, properly maintained litter box is essential for your cat's well-being and contributes to a harmonious home environment.

# CHAPTER 9

# GROOMING YOUR RAGDOLL CAT

## Brushing

Brushing your Ragdoll cat is a fundamental aspect of grooming due to their long, luxurious fur, which can be prone to matting and tangling. Regular brushing not only helps maintain their coat's appearance but also promotes their overall health.

### **Daily Brushing**
To keep your Ragdoll's coat in top condition, aim to brush them daily. This routine helps remove loose hair, dirt, and debris, preventing mats from forming. It also distributes natural oils throughout the fur, which enhances its shine and

reduces shedding. Use a slicker brush with fine, bent wires to gently work through the fur, starting at the roots and moving towards the tips. This method helps untangle any knots and ensures a smooth coat.

### *Dealing with Mats and Tangles*

Mats and tangles are common in Ragdoll cats due to their semi-long fur. If you encounter a mat, use your fingers to gently separate the fur before using a mat comb or a detangling brush. For persistent mats, a dematting tool or comb with rotating blades can be effective. Be patient and avoid pulling on the fur, as this can be painful for your cat. For severe matting, you might need to carefully cut out the mats using grooming scissors. Always cut away from the skin to avoid accidents.

### *Tools for Brushing*

Invest in high-quality grooming tools suited for long-haired cats. A slicker brush is excellent for removing loose hair and detangling, while a wide-toothed comb helps manage larger knots and mats. Additionally, a grooming rake can be useful for removing undercoat fur, especially during shedding seasons. Clean your grooming tools regularly to remove hair and prevent the buildup of dirt.

### *Additional Tips*
Make brushing a positive experience by associating it with treats and praise. Start with short brushing sessions and gradually increase the duration as your Ragdoll becomes more comfortable. Regular brushing not only prevents tangles but also helps you keep an eye out for any skin issues or parasites that may require veterinary attention.

## Bathing

Bathing your Ragdoll cat is generally not necessary on a frequent basis due to their natural grooming abilities. However, occasional baths can help manage shedding, remove dirt, and keep their coat in good condition.

### *Frequency*
Most Ragdolls only need a bath every few

months, but this can vary based on their activity level and how dirty they get. Overbathing can strip the fur of natural oils, leading to dryness and irritation. Adjust the bathing schedule according to your cat's needs and consult with your veterinarian if you're unsure.

### *Preparing for a Bath*

Before bathing your Ragdoll, gather all necessary supplies, including cat-specific shampoo, a towel, and a non-slip mat for the bathtub or sink. Brush your cat thoroughly to remove loose hair and tangles, as this will make the bathing process smoother and more effective.

### *Bathing Technique*

Fill the bathtub or sink with lukewarm water, ensuring it is not too hot or cold. Gently place your Ragdoll in the water, supporting their body to prevent slipping. Use a cup or a gentle spray nozzle to wet their fur, avoiding the head. Apply a small amount of cat-specific shampoo, lathering it gently. Avoid getting shampoo in their eyes, ears, or mouth. Rinse thoroughly to remove all soap residue, which can cause skin irritation if left behind.

### *Drying*
After the bath, wrap your Ragdoll in a towel to absorb excess water. Gently pat their fur dry, avoiding vigorous rubbing, which can lead to tangles. If your cat is comfortable with it, use a hairdryer on a low, cool setting to help dry their fur. Keep the hairdryer at a safe distance and avoid overheating. Alternatively, allow your Ragdoll to air dry in a warm, draft-free environment.

### *Additional Considerations*
Monitor your Ragdoll for signs of stress or discomfort during the bath. Use soothing tones and offer treats to create a positive association. If your cat becomes too anxious, consider bathing them more frequently to help them acclimate or consult a professional groomer for assistance.

## *Trimming or Clipping*

Trimming or clipping your Ragdoll's fur helps manage its length and keeps it looking neat. While Ragdolls generally don't require extensive clipping, occasional grooming is important for their comfort and hygiene.

### *Tools and Techniques*
For trimming, use grooming scissors or clippers designed for cats. Trim around the paws, belly, and any areas prone to matting. Be particularly cautious around sensitive areas like the tail and underarms. Use clippers with safety features or rounded tips to minimize the risk of cutting the skin. Trim in small increments and regularly check to ensure you're not cutting too close to the skin.

### *Handling Matting*
If your Ragdoll's fur becomes severely matted, clipping may be necessary. Carefully use clippers or scissors to remove the mats, cutting away from the skin to avoid injury. For large mats, consider seeking professional help to avoid causing pain or discomfort to your cat.

*Professional Grooming*

Some Ragdoll owners opt for professional grooming services to manage their cat's coat. Professional groomers have the expertise and equipment to handle complex grooming tasks, including severe matting and extensive coat management. Regular professional grooming can be a convenient option for maintaining your Ragdoll's appearance.

*Additional Tips*

When trimming or clipping, ensure your Ragdoll is calm and comfortable. Use treats and positive reinforcement to make the experience pleasant. If your cat is particularly anxious about grooming, consider gradual desensitization or consulting a professional groomer for guidance.

## Nail Care

Maintaining your Ragdoll's nails is an essential part of their grooming routine. Regular nail care prevents overgrowth and reduces the risk of injury or health issues.

### *Frequency*
Check your Ragdoll's nails weekly and trim them as needed. Most cats' nails grow quickly and can become sharp or uncomfortable if not managed regularly. Aim to trim the nails every 1-2 weeks to keep them at a healthy length.

### *Trimming Technique*
Use cat-specific nail clippers or scissor-type clippers for trimming. Gently press on your Ragdoll's paw pad to extend the claws and trim the sharp tips. Avoid cutting into the quick, pink area of the nail that contains blood vessels and nerves. If you're unsure, trim only a small amount at a time to prevent bleeding and discomfort.

### *Dealing with Anxiety*
If your Ragdoll is anxious about nail trimming, make the experience as positive as possible. Use treats and gentle praise to reward calm behavior. Start with short, frequent sessions to help your

cat become accustomed to the process. If necessary, seek assistance from a veterinarian or professional groomer.

### *Additional Tips*
Ensure you have a comfortable and well-lit space for nail trimming. Use distraction techniques, such as toys or treats, to keep your Ragdoll engaged and relaxed. Regular nail care helps prevent issues like ingrown nails or nail splits, which can cause pain and discomfort.

## Ear and Eye Care

Regular ear and eye care is crucial for preventing infections and maintaining your Ragdoll's health. Regular checkups and cleanings help keep these areas in good condition.

### *Ear Care*
Inspect your Ragdoll's ears weekly for signs of dirt, wax buildup, or infection. Gently wipe the outer part of the ear with a cotton ball or gauze dampened with a cat-safe ear cleaner. Avoid

inserting anything into the ear canal, as this can cause damage. If you notice redness, swelling, or a foul odor, consult your veterinarian for further evaluation.

### *Eye Care*
Monitor your Ragdoll's eyes for any signs of discharge, redness, or irritation. Gently clean any discharge using a soft, damp cloth or cotton ball. Avoid using harsh chemicals or products not specifically designed for cats. If your cat has persistent eye problems or abnormal discharge, seek veterinary advice to address potential infections or other issues.

### *Additional Tips*
Maintaining a clean environment can help reduce the risk of ear and eye infections. Regularly clean your Ragdoll's bedding and grooming tools to minimize exposure to allergens and irritants. If you notice any signs of discomfort or unusual symptoms, consult your veterinarian for appropriate care.

## *Finding a Groomer*

Finding a qualified groomer can be beneficial for managing your Ragdoll's grooming needs. A professional groomer can help with tasks that may be challenging to handle at home and ensure your cat receives proper care.

### *Experience with Long-Haired Cats*
Look for groomers who have experience with long-haired breeds like Ragdolls. They will be familiar with the specific grooming techniques required for managing a Ragdoll's coat and handling issues such as matting and tangling.

### *Reputation and Recommendations*
Seek recommendations from other cat owners or veterinarians. Reading reviews and asking for references can help you find a reputable groomer who provides quality care. A good groomer will have positive feedback from satisfied clients and demonstrate a caring, professional attitude.

### *Grooming Services*
Verify the services offered by the groomer, including brushing, bathing, trimming, and nail

care. Discuss your Ragdoll's specific grooming needs and preferences to ensure they are addressed. A thorough discussion about your cat's grooming requirements will help the groomer tailor their services to meet your needs.

### *Comfort and Safety*

Visit the grooming facility to assess its cleanliness and the comfort of the environment. Ensure that the groomer uses safe and appropriate equipment and that they handle your Ragdoll with care. A good groomer will prioritize your cat's comfort and safety, providing a stress-free grooming experience. By understanding and addressing these aspects of grooming.

# CHAPTER 10

## FEEDING YOUR RAGDOLL

### Benefits of Quality Nutrition

Providing your Ragdoll with high-quality nutrition is crucial for their health and well-being. A balanced diet not only supports their physical health but also contributes to their overall quality of life.

*<u>Overall Health and Longevity</u>*
The right nutrition is foundational to preventing many common health issues in cats. A diet rich in essential nutrients helps maintain a healthy weight, supports organ function, and can help prevent diseases like diabetes, kidney disease, and heart problems. By ensuring that your Ragdoll receives the proper balance of vitamins,

minerals, and other nutrients, you contribute to their overall longevity and reduce the risk of chronic health issues. Quality nutrition supports the immune system, making it easier for your Ragdoll to fight off infections and diseases.

### *Healthy Skin and Coat*

The health of your Ragdoll's coat is often a reflection of their diet. Essential fatty acids, such as omega-3 and omega-6, play a critical role in maintaining a glossy coat and healthy skin. These nutrients help to keep the coat soft and shiny, and they can reduce shedding and dandruff. A lack of these essential fatty acids can lead to a dry, brittle coat and skin issues such as itching and inflammation. Regular intake of these nutrients helps to promote a well-hydrated and lustrous coat, enhancing your Ragdoll's appearance and comfort.

### *Energy Levels and Vitality*

A diet that provides the right balance of proteins, fats, and carbohydrates ensures that your Ragdoll has the energy needed for their daily activities. Cats, especially those who are active or playful, require a diet that supports their high energy levels. Proper nutrition helps in maintaining their muscle mass and supports their overall vitality. If your Ragdoll is not getting enough energy from their food, they may become lethargic or less engaged in activities. Ensuring they have a well-balanced diet helps to maintain their enthusiasm for play and interaction.

## ***Digestive Health***

The right balance of nutrients and fiber in your Ragdoll's diet supports healthy digestion. Fiber aids in the prevention of common digestive issues such as constipation or diarrhea. Additionally, a diet rich in prebiotics and probiotics can enhance gut health by promoting the growth of beneficial bacteria. Healthy digestion ensures that your Ragdoll absorbs essential nutrients effectively, which contributes to their overall health. Proper digestion also minimizes gastrointestinal discomfort, leading to a happier and more comfortable cat.

### *Weight Management*

Maintaining a healthy weight is crucial for your Ragdoll's health. Obesity can lead to numerous health problems, including diabetes, arthritis, and reduced lifespan. A balanced diet helps regulate their weight by providing the right amount of calories and nutrients. High-quality food with appropriate protein and fat levels supports lean muscle mass while controlling fat accumulation. Regular monitoring of your Ragdoll's weight and adjusting their food intake as needed can help prevent obesity and related health issues.

## *Commercial Diets*

Commercial cat foods are a convenient option and are designed to meet the nutritional needs of cats. They come in various types, including dry kibble, canned food, and semi-moist food, each with its own benefits and considerations.

### *Dry Kibble*

Dry kibble is a common choice for cat owners due to its convenience and long shelf life. It's easier to store and can be left out for your Ragdoll to graze on throughout the day. The crunchy texture of kibble helps reduce plaque buildup on your cat's teeth, potentially improving dental health. However, not all dry foods are created equal. Choose high-quality kibble with meat as the primary ingredient and avoid those with excessive fillers like corn or wheat. High-quality kibble will provide balanced nutrition without unnecessary additives.

### *Canned Food*

Canned food is often recommended for its higher moisture content, which helps keep your Ragdoll hydrated. The increased moisture can be particularly beneficial for cats that are prone to urinary tract issues or those that don't drink enough water. Canned food is generally more palatable and may be preferred by picky eaters. Look for canned foods that list meat or fish as the first ingredient and have a good balance of protein and fat. Be cautious of brands that include artificial colors or preservatives.

### _Semi-Moist Food_

Semi-moist foods have a texture between dry kibble and canned food, and while they can be appealing to some cats, they often contain higher levels of sugar and salt. These added ingredients are not necessary for your Ragdoll's diet and can contribute to health issues such as obesity and hypertension. If you choose semi-moist food, carefully review the ingredient list and ensure it provides balanced nutrition without excessive sugar or salt.

### _Choosing the Right Brand_

Selecting the right commercial diet involves researching and choosing brands that meet high-quality standards. Look for brands with a reputation for safety and quality, and check that the food meets the standards set by the Association of American Feed Control Officials (AAFCO). AAFCO certification ensures that the food provides complete and balanced nutrition for cats. Consult with your veterinarian to identify the best brand and formula for your

Ragdoll's specific health needs and dietary preferences.

## *Homemade Diets*

Homemade diets provide the advantage of tailoring meals to your Ragdoll's specific needs and preferences. However, they require careful planning to ensure they meet all of your cat's nutritional requirements.

### **_Benefits of Homemade Diets_**
Homemade diets offer control over ingredients, allowing you to avoid artificial additives and choose high-quality, fresh ingredients. This can be particularly beneficial if your Ragdoll has specific dietary sensitivities or allergies. Homemade meals can also be customized to suit your cat's taste preferences, potentially making mealtimes more enjoyable for them.
Additionally, preparing food at home allows you to monitor ingredient quality and avoid potential contaminants.

## *Nutritional Balance*

Cats have unique dietary needs, and a balanced homemade diet must include the right proportions of proteins, fats, carbohydrates, vitamins, and minerals. Essential nutrients such as taurine, arginine, and arachidonic acid must be included to meet your Ragdoll's needs. Consulting with a veterinarian or a pet nutritionist is crucial to create a diet that provides complete nutrition. Supplementing homemade meals with appropriate vitamins and minerals may be necessary to ensure a balanced diet.

## *Preparation and Safety*

When preparing homemade meals, use fresh, high-quality ingredients and ensure proper food safety practices. Avoid using ingredients that are toxic to cats, such as onions, garlic, or certain spices. Cook meats thoroughly to prevent bacterial contamination and avoid using bones that can pose a choking hazard. Proper handling and storage of homemade food are essential to prevent spoilage and maintain nutritional quality.

### *Consultation and Monitoring*
Regular consultations with your veterinarian are important when feeding a homemade diet. Your vet can help monitor your Ragdoll's health and adjust their diet as needed. Periodic blood tests can help assess nutritional adequacy and identify any deficiencies. Be prepared to make adjustments based on your cat's health status and changing needs. A well-balanced homemade diet, along with regular veterinary check-ups, can support your Ragdoll's long-term health.

## *Ingredients to Avoid*

Certain ingredients can be harmful to cats and should be avoided to ensure your Ragdoll's health and safety. Being aware of these ingredients helps you make informed choices about their diet.

### *Toxic Ingredients*
Some common foods and ingredients are toxic to cats and can cause serious health problems. These include onions, garlic, chives, and leeks, which can lead to gastrointestinal upset, anemia,

and more severe health issues. Chocolate, caffeine, and alcohol are also highly toxic and can cause poisoning or even be fatal. Ensure that your Ragdoll's food does not contain these harmful substances.

### *Artificial Additives*
Avoid foods that contain artificial colors, flavors, and preservatives. These additives may not contribute to your cat's nutritional needs and can potentially cause allergic reactions or sensitivities. Choose foods with natural ingredients and minimal processing to ensure your Ragdoll's diet is as healthy as possible. Natural ingredients and limited additives contribute to better overall health and reduce the risk of adverse reactions.

### *High-Carbohydrate Ingredients*
Cats are obligate carnivores and require a diet high in protein rather than carbohydrates. Foods with excessive carbohydrates, such as grains and fillers, can lead to obesity and diabetes. Look for diets where meat or fish is the primary ingredient and avoid those with excessive fillers

like corn or wheat. High-quality cat food should be rich in protein and low in unnecessary carbohydrates.

### *Excessive Salt and Sugar*
Foods high in salt or sugar can contribute to health problems such as hypertension and diabetes. Cats do not need added sugars or excessive salt in their diet. Always check the nutritional information and ingredient list to ensure that the food you choose does not contain high levels of these potentially harmful substances. Opt for foods with moderate salt levels and no added sugars to support your Ragdoll's health.

Proper nutrition is key to your Ragdoll's health and well-being. By choosing quality commercial diets or preparing balanced homemade meals, and by avoiding harmful ingredients, you can help ensure that your feline friend remains healthy and happy throughout their lifes.

# CHAPTER 11

## YOUR RAGDOLL'S HEALTH CARE

### Choosing a Vet

Choosing the right veterinarian for your Ragdoll is a crucial step in ensuring their overall health and well-being. A good vet will not only provide medical care but also serve as a partner in maintaining your cat's health throughout their life.

#### Research and Recommendations

Start by researching veterinarians in your area and seeking recommendations from friends, family, or local cat breeders. Online reviews and veterinary associations can provide additional insights into the reputation and quality of care offered by different clinics. Consider visiting a few clinics to observe the facilities and meet the staff before making a decision.

### *Experience and Specialization*

Look for a veterinarian with experience and specialization in feline care. Cats have unique health needs compared to other pets, and a vet with a strong background in feline medicine will be better equipped to address these needs. Check if the vet is a member of professional organizations such as the American Association of Feline Practitioners (AAFP), which indicates a commitment to high standards in feline health care.

### *Communication and Comfort*

Choose a vet with whom you feel comfortable communicating. Effective communication is essential for discussing your Ragdoll's health concerns, treatment options, and preventive care. A good vet should listen to your questions, provide clear explanations, and involve you in decision-making regarding your cat's health.

### *Emergency Care*

Ensure that the veterinary clinic offers

emergency care or has a partnership with an emergency veterinary hospital. Accidents and health issues can arise unexpectedly, and having access to emergency services is crucial for timely treatment. Inquire about the clinic's emergency protocols and their approach to after-hours care.

## *Microchipping*

Microchipping is a vital step in ensuring the safety and recovery of your Ragdoll if they become lost. This small, electronic device provides a permanent form of identification that can help reunite you with your pet.

### *What is Microchipping?*
A microchip is a tiny, glass-encased device about the size of a grain of rice. It is implanted under your cat's skin, usually between the shoulder blades, and contains a unique identification number. This number is registered in a database along with your contact information. If your Ragdoll is found and taken to a vet or animal shelter, the microchip can be

scanned to access your contact details and facilitate a quick reunion.

### *Benefits of Microchipping*

Microchipping offers several advantages over traditional identification methods, such as collars and tags. Unlike collars, which can be lost or removed, microchips are permanent and tamper-proof. They provide a reliable way to identify your cat, even if they lose their collar or tag. Microchips also offer peace of mind, knowing that there is a backup identification method if your Ragdoll goes missing.

### *Microchip Registration*

After microchipping, it is essential to register the chip with the manufacturer's database and keep your contact information up to date. If you move or change phone numbers, update the information in the database to ensure that you can be reached if your Ragdoll is found. Many microchip companies offer online registration and easy updates, making it simple to keep your information current.

## *Vaccinations*

Vaccinations are a fundamental aspect of preventive health care for your Ragdoll. They help protect your cat from various infectious diseases and contribute to their overall well-being.

### *Core Vaccines*

Core vaccines are recommended for all cats and provide protection against serious and potentially life-threatening diseases. For Ragdolls, these typically include vaccines for feline viral rhinotracheitis (FVR), calicivirus, and panleukopenia (FPV), commonly referred to as the FVRCP vaccine. Additionally, the rabies vaccine is crucial for preventing rabies, a fatal viral disease that can be transmitted to humans.

### *Non-Core Vaccines*

Non-core vaccines are given based on your cat's risk factors and lifestyle. These may include vaccines for feline leukemia virus (FeLV) and feline immunodeficiency virus (FIV). The FeLV vaccine is particularly important for outdoor or multi-cat households, as FeLV can be transmitted through direct contact with infected cats. The FIV vaccine may be recommended for cats at higher risk of exposure to FIV-positive cats.

### *Vaccination Schedule*

Kittens typically start their vaccination series around 6 to 8 weeks of age, with booster shots given every 3 to 4 weeks until they are about 16 weeks old. After the initial series, your Ragdoll will need periodic booster shots to maintain immunity. Your veterinarian will provide a vaccination schedule tailored to your cat's needs and lifestyle.

## Parasite Prevention

Parasite prevention is essential for keeping your Ragdoll healthy and free from common parasites such as fleas, ticks, and worms. Effective prevention helps avoid discomfort and potential health issues associated with parasitic infections.

### *Fleas and Ticks*

Fleas and ticks are common external parasites that can cause itching, skin infections, and discomfort. Flea prevention can be achieved with monthly topical treatments or oral medications, while tick prevention often involves similar treatments. Discuss with your veterinarian the best options for your Ragdoll based on their lifestyle and exposure risk.

### *Internal Parasites*

Internal parasites, such as roundworms, hookworms, and tapeworms, can cause gastrointestinal issues and other health problems. Regular deworming is essential, especially for kittens and cats with outdoor access. Your vet can recommend appropriate deworming treatments and schedules based on your cat's specific needs.

### *Heartworm Prevention*

Heartworm disease, although less common in cats than in dogs, can still occur. It is transmitted by mosquitoes and can cause serious health issues. Preventive medications for heartworms are available and can be discussed with your veterinarian. Regular check-ups and testing can help detect any potential issues early.

## *Spaying and Neutering*

Spaying and neutering are important aspects of responsible pet ownership that contribute to the health and well-being of your Ragdoll.

### *Benefits of Spaying and Neutering*
Spaying (removal of ovaries and uterus in females) and neutering (removal of testicles in males) offer several health benefits. Spaying reduces the risk of uterine infections and breast cancer, while neutering helps prevent testicular cancer and reduces the risk of prostate issues. Both procedures can also help prevent behavioral issues related to mating instincts, such as aggression and marking territory.

### *Timing*
The optimal time for spaying or neutering is usually around 5 to 6 months of age, although this can vary based on your cat's health and development. Consult with your veterinarian to determine the best timing for your Ragdoll. Early spaying or neutering can help avoid

unwanted litters and reduce the risk of certain health problems.

### *Recovery and Care*
After the procedure, your Ragdoll will need some time to recover. Follow your veterinarian's post-operative care instructions, which may include keeping your cat indoors, monitoring the surgical site for signs of infection, and limiting physical activity. Most cats recover quickly and return to their normal activities within a few days.

## *Declawing*

Declawing is a controversial procedure that involves the amputation of the last bone of each toe. It is important to understand the implications of declawing and consider alternative solutions for managing scratching behavior.

### *Understanding Declawing*
Declawing is not a simple nail trim; it involves the removal of bone and tissue, which can lead

to pain and behavioral changes. Many veterinarians and animal welfare organizations view declawing as an inhumane procedure due to its potential for long-term physical and psychological effects. Alternatives, such as providing scratching posts or using nail caps, are recommended to address scratching behavior without resorting to declawing.

### *Alternatives to Declawing*

Provide your Ragdoll with appropriate scratching posts and pads to satisfy their natural scratching instincts. Regular nail trimming and the use of soft nail caps can also help minimize damage to furniture and reduce the need for declawing. Consult with your veterinarian for advice on managing scratching behavior and maintaining your cat's claws.

## Common Genetic Conditions

Ragdolls are generally healthy cats, but like all breeds, they are prone to certain genetic conditions. Being aware of these conditions can help you monitor your cat's health and seek early intervention if needed.

## *Hypertrophic Cardiomyopathy (HCM)*

HCM is a common heart condition in Ragdolls that involves thickening of the heart muscle. It can lead to heart failure and other complications. Regular veterinary check-ups and screenings can help detect HCM early and manage the condition effectively.

## *Polycystic Kidney Disease (PKD)*

PKD is a genetic condition characterized by the formation of fluid-filled cysts in the kidneys. It can lead to kidney dysfunction and renal failure. Regular veterinary examinations and monitoring can help manage PKD and ensure your Ragdoll's kidney health.

## *Other Genetic Conditions*

Other genetic conditions that may affect Ragdolls include dental issues and certain eye problems. Regular vet visits and health screenings can help identify and manage these conditions early. Consult with your veterinarian for guidance on maintaining your Ragdoll's health and addressing any breed-specific concerns.

## Pet Insurance

Pet insurance is a valuable tool for managing the costs of veterinary care and ensuring that your Ragdoll receives the best possible treatment in case of illness or injury.

### Types of Coverage

Pet insurance policies vary in coverage, with options including accident-only plans, illness-only plans, and comprehensive plans that cover both accidents and illnesses. Some policies also offer coverage for routine care, such as vaccinations and dental cleanings. Choose a plan that aligns with your needs and budget, and carefully review the policy details, including coverage limits, deductibles, and exclusions.

### Benefits of Pet Insurance

Pet insurance can help alleviate the financial burden of unexpected veterinary expenses, allowing you to focus on your Ragdoll's care rather than.

# CHAPTER 12

## TRAVELING WITH YOUR RAGDOLL CAT

### Car Travel

Traveling by car with your Ragdoll cat can be a smooth experience if you plan ahead and follow some key practices to ensure their safety and comfort.

**<u>Preparing for the Journey</u>**
Before embarking on a car trip, it's important to prepare your Ragdoll for the journey. Begin by getting your cat accustomed to their carrier, which should be well-ventilated and spacious enough for them to stand and turn around comfortably. Place familiar bedding or toys inside to create a sense of security. Allow your cat to explore the carrier before the trip so they

become accustomed to it. For long trips, consider taking your Ragdoll for short car rides to help them get used to the motion and sounds of the vehicle.

### *Safety Measures*
Ensure your Ragdoll is safely secured during the trip. Using a pet seatbelt harness or securing the carrier with a seatbelt can prevent the carrier from moving around in case of sudden stops or sharp turns. Avoid letting your cat roam freely in the car, as this can be distracting for the driver and potentially dangerous for your cat. Keep the windows closed or cracked just slightly to prevent your Ragdoll from escaping if they become agitated.

### *Comfort and Well-being*
Maintain a comfortable environment for your Ragdoll by keeping the car at a moderate temperature. Provide fresh water and a small amount of food if the trip is long, but avoid feeding your cat right before departure to minimize the risk of motion sickness. Make frequent stops during longer trips to check on

your cat and offer them a chance to stretch and use the litter box if needed. A calming pheromone spray or an anxiety-reducing product may help if your Ragdoll is particularly nervous about traveling.

### *Emergency Preparedness*
Carry a basic pet first aid kit and your Ragdoll's health records, including vaccination history and any medical information, in case of emergencies. Familiarize yourself with the locations of veterinary clinics along your route in case your Ragdoll requires medical attention. Having a plan in place for emergencies can help reduce stress and ensure your cat receives prompt care if needed.

## *Air Travel*

Air travel with your Ragdoll requires careful planning and adherence to airline regulations to ensure a smooth journey.

### *Choosing the Right Carrier*
When flying with your Ragdoll, select an

airline-approved carrier that meets the airline's size and design requirements. The carrier should be well-ventilated, sturdy, and comfortable for your cat. Include familiar items such as their bedding or a favorite toy to provide comfort during the flight. Check with your airline for specific guidelines on carrier dimensions and any additional requirements for traveling with pets.

### *Preparing for Security*
At the airport security checkpoint, you will likely need to remove your Ragdoll from their carrier and carry them through the metal detector while the carrier is screened separately. Ensure your cat is securely held or in a harness to prevent them from escaping. Be prepared for the possibility of a full-body scan or additional screening if required.

### *During the Flight*
If your Ragdoll will be traveling in the cabin with you, keep them calm by speaking to them soothingly and offering treats or toys. Avoid opening the carrier during the flight, as this can

lead to stress or escape. If your Ragdoll will be traveling in the cargo hold, ensure that the carrier is well-marked with your contact information and any special instructions for handling. Choose a direct flight if possible to minimize travel time and reduce stress.

### *Post-Arrival Care*

Upon arrival, check on your Ragdoll immediately and ensure they are safe and comfortable. Offer them water and a small amount of food if appropriate. Allow them time to adjust to their new environment and be prepared for potential signs of stress or discomfort. If your Ragdoll exhibits any concerning symptoms or behaviors, consult with a veterinarian as soon as possible.

## Cat-Friendly Accommodations

Finding cat-friendly accommodations is essential for a stress-free trip with your Ragdoll. Many options cater to traveling pets and provide amenities that make your stay comfortable for both you and your cat.

### *Research and Booking*

When booking accommodations, look for pet-friendly hotels, vacation rentals, or Airbnb properties that explicitly welcome cats. Read reviews from other pet owners to ensure the property is genuinely cat-friendly and that there are no hidden fees or restrictions. Some accommodations may offer additional amenities such as pet beds, litter boxes, or enclosed outdoor areas.

### *Preparing Your Cat for a New Environment*

Before arriving at your accommodation, prepare your Ragdoll for the new environment by bringing familiar items such as their bed, toys, and litter box. Set up a designated area in the accommodation where your cat can feel secure and have access to their essentials. Gradually introduce your Ragdoll to the new space and monitor their behavior to ensure they are comfortable.

### *Safety and Comfort*

Ensure that the accommodation is safe for your Ragdoll by checking for potential hazards such as open windows, accessible electrical cords, or toxic plants. Keep your cat's food and water dishes, litter box, and scratching post accessible to make them feel at home. Maintain a routine as much as possible to provide stability and reduce stress.

### *Emergency Contacts*

Identify nearby veterinary clinics and pet emergency services in case of any health issues or emergencies during your stay. Keep a list of contact information for local veterinarians and pet services readily available. Having this information on hand ensures you are prepared for any unforeseen circumstances and can address any health concerns promptly.

## *Leaving Your Cat Behind*

If traveling without your Ragdoll, it's important to make arrangements for their care to ensure they remain happy and healthy while you are away.

### *Choosing a Caregiver*

Consider the options for your Ragdoll's care while you're away, such as hiring a pet sitter, using a boarding facility, or asking a trusted friend or family member to look after them. Ensure that the caregiver is familiar with Ragdoll cats and understands their specific needs and preferences. Conduct interviews or visits to assess the caregiver's suitability and to provide them with instructions for your cat's care.

### *Preparing for Their Absence*

Prepare your Ragdoll for your absence by gradually acclimating them to the caregiver or boarding facility. Leave detailed instructions about their feeding schedule, medication needs, and any special requirements. Provide the caregiver with your contact information and emergency contacts, including the name and contact details of your veterinarian.

### *Comfort and Familiarity*

To ease your Ragdoll's transition while you are away, leave familiar items such as their bed, toys, and bedding with them. These items can provide comfort and reduce anxiety by maintaining a sense of normalcy. Ensure that their environment remains stable and consistent, and avoid making major changes right before your departure.

### *Monitoring and Communication*
Stay in touch with the caregiver to receive updates on your Ragdoll's well-being. Many boarding facilities offer webcams or regular updates to keep you informed about your cat's condition. If possible, arrange for video calls or phone calls to reassure your Ragdoll that you are still present and to ease any separation anxiety.

Traveling with your Ragdoll or leaving them behind can be managed effectively with proper planning and preparation. By taking the necessary steps to ensure their safety, comfort, and well-being, you can enjoy your travels while ensuring your feline companion remains happy and healthy.

# CHAPTER 13

# INTO THE WORLD OF SHOWING

## All About Cat Shows

cat's physical attributes, such as their body structure, head shape, and eye color. Each breed has its own standard, which outlines the ideal characteristics and traits for that breed. Judges use these standards to determine how closely each cat conforms to the breed ideal.

### Categories and Awards

Cat shows are divided into different categories based on breed, age, and gender. Awards are given for various placements, including Best in Breed, Best in Show, and various other titles depending on the level of competition. Cats may also be recognized for their behavior, grooming, and overall presentation. Awards and titles can enhance a cat's reputation and contribute to their breeder's and owner's prestige within the feline community.

### *Preparation and Participation*

Preparing for a cat show involves grooming, training, and familiarizing your Ragdoll with the show environment. Owners should ensure their cats are in optimal condition, including a clean and well-maintained coat, trimmed nails, and overall good health. Socializing your cat to handle the stress of the show environment is also important. This includes exposure to different people, sounds, and sights that they may encounter during the event. Participating in a cat show can be a rewarding experience that provides recognition for the hard work and dedication involved in caring for and presenting your Ragdoll.

## *Ragdoll Breed Standards*

The Ragdoll breed standard outlines the ideal physical characteristics and temperament for Ragdolls as recognized by cat fancier organizations. Understanding these standards is crucial for those interested in showing Ragdolls and ensuring their cats meet the criteria for competition.

## *Physical Characteristics*
Ragdolls are known for their large size, semi-long coat, and striking blue eyes. The breed standard specifies several key attributes:

- ***Body***: Ragdolls are large, muscular cats with a rectangular body shape and a sturdy bone structure. They have a broad chest, strong legs, and a bushy tail. The breed standard emphasizes a balanced and proportionate body with a graceful appearance.
- ***Head:*** The head should be a modified wedge shape with a gentle contour. Ragdolls have a rounded forehead, a well-defined nose, and a strong chin. Their cheeks are full, and their muzzle is moderately rounded.
- ***Eyes:*** Ragdolls have large, oval-shaped eyes that are set slightly oblique and are a deep, vivid blue. The eyes should be

well-spaced and expressive, contributing to the breed's sweet and gentle appearance.
- *Coat*: The coat is semi-long, plush, and silky with a soft texture. Ragdolls have a dense undercoat and a longer, flowing topcoat that lies flat against the body. The coat color and pattern are significant aspects of the breed standard, with Ragdolls typically exhibiting color points similar to those of Siamese cats. Common colors include seal, blue, chocolate, lilac, and their respective point patterns (e.g., color point, bicolor, and mitted).

## *Temperament and Personality*

The Ragdoll breed standard also describes the ideal temperament of the breed. Ragdolls are known for their docile, calm, and affectionate nature. They are often described as "puppy-like" due to their tendency to follow their owners around and seek out human interaction. Ragdolls are generally friendly with children and other pets, making them well-suited for family environments.

### *Breed Variations and Faults*

While the breed standard provides a detailed description of the ideal Ragdoll, there are variations and potential faults that may affect a cat's show performance. Variations within the breed include different coat colors and patterns, which are judged according to their adherence to the standard. Faults, such as deviations from the ideal body structure, coat quality, or eye color, may impact a cat's placement in the show ring. Understanding these aspects can help breeders and owners evaluate their cats and make improvements if necessary.

## *Getting Started in Cat Shows*

Getting started in cat shows involves a combination of preparation, knowledge, and involvement in the feline community. For those new to the world of cat showing, the following steps can help facilitate a successful entry into the competitive arena.

### *Research and Education*

Before entering a cat show, it is essential to educate yourself about the process and requirements. Research different cat shows and organizations to find events that align with your interests and goals. Learn about the specific breed standards for Ragdolls and familiarize yourself with the judging criteria. Attending local cat shows as a spectator can provide valuable insights into the environment and the expectations for participants.

### *Grooming and Training*

Proper grooming and training are crucial for a successful showing experience. Ensure your Ragdoll is in top condition, with a well-groomed coat, clean ears, trimmed nails, and a healthy appearance. Training your cat to handle the show environment, including exposure to different people, noises, and handling, will help reduce stress and improve their performance. Socializing your Ragdoll with various stimuli and practicing handling techniques can contribute to a positive show experience.

### _Finding a Mentor_

Connecting with experienced breeders or show participants can provide valuable guidance and support. A mentor can offer advice on show preparation, handling techniques, and the nuances of the judging process. Joining feline clubs or organizations can also provide networking opportunities and access to resources that can help you navigate the world of cat showing.

### _Entering a Show_

To enter a cat show, you will need to complete the registration process, which typically involves submitting an entry form and paying the entry fee. Review the show's rules and guidelines to ensure you comply with all requirements. Prepare for the event by packing necessary supplies, including grooming tools, food, water, and any documentation required by the show organizers.

### _Participating and Learning_

Participating in cat shows is a learning experience that offers opportunities for growth and improvement. Pay attention to feedback from judges and other participants, and use this information to enhance your Ragdoll's presentation and performance. Engaging with the cat show community and continuing to educate yourself about breed standards and show techniques will contribute to your success in the world of feline competition.

By understanding the intricacies of cat shows, adhering to breed standards, and preparing thoroughly, you can enjoy a rewarding experience in showcasing your Ragdoll and contributing to the celebration of feline excellence.

# CHAPTER 14

## YOUR AGING RAGDOLL CAT

### Common Signs of Aging

As your Ragdoll cat matures, you may observe various signs that indicate they are entering their senior years. Recognizing these signs is essential for providing appropriate care and ensuring their continued comfort and well-being.

***Physical Changes***
One of the most noticeable signs of aging in cats is a change in physical appearance. Senior Ragdolls may exhibit a graying or thinning coat, which is a natural part of the aging process. Their fur may also become less dense and lose some of its luster. Additionally, you may notice a decrease in muscle mass, leading to a more prominent skeletal structure. Weight loss or gain

can also occur, often due to changes in metabolism or activity levels.

### *Changes in Mobility*
Arthritis and joint stiffness are common in aging cats. You may observe your Ragdoll moving more slowly or having difficulty jumping or climbing. They might also show signs of discomfort when getting up or lying down. Watch for changes in their gait or reluctance to engage in activities they once enjoyed. These changes can significantly affect their quality of life and may require adjustments to their environment or care routine.

### *Behavioral Changes*
Senior Ragdolls may experience changes in behavior as they age. Increased vocalization, altered sleeping patterns, or a decrease in activity levels can be signs of aging. Your cat might also become more irritable or seek out more attention and comfort. Cognitive decline is another possibility, which can manifest as disorientation or confusion. Keeping an eye on these behavioral changes will help you address

any underlying issues and provide appropriate support.

### *Health Indicators*
Changes in appetite, water intake, and litter box habits can signal underlying health issues in senior cats. A decrease in appetite or sudden weight loss may indicate dental problems, kidney disease, or other health concerns. Increased thirst or urination could be a sign of diabetes or kidney disease. Regular monitoring and veterinary check-ups are crucial for identifying and managing any health issues early.

## *Basic Senior Cat Care*

Caring for a senior Ragdoll requires special attention to ensure their comfort and health. Adapting your care routine to their changing needs can help enhance their quality of life as they age.

### *Comfortable Environment*
Create a comfortable and accessible environment

for your aging Ragdoll. Provide soft, supportive bedding that is easy for them to get in and out of. Ensure that their litter box is easily accessible and consider using a low-sided box to accommodate any mobility issues. Place their food and water dishes in a location that is easy for them to reach without having to climb or jump.

### *Routine and Adaptations*
Maintain a consistent routine to provide stability and reduce stress for your senior cat. Regular feeding times and a predictable daily schedule can help your Ragdoll feel secure. Make adaptations to your home to accommodate any mobility issues, such as adding ramps or steps to help them reach their favorite spots. Avoid sudden changes or disruptions that could cause anxiety.

### *Healthcare Monitoring*
Regular veterinary check-ups are essential for monitoring your senior Ragdoll's health. Schedule routine visits to assess their overall condition, address any health concerns, and

update vaccinations or preventative treatments as needed. Discuss any changes in behavior, appetite, or physical condition with your veterinarian to ensure timely intervention and management of health issues.

### ***Grooming and Hygiene***
Senior cats may require additional grooming and hygiene care. Their coats might need more frequent brushing to prevent matting and reduce hairballs. Check their ears regularly for signs of infection or wax buildup, and clean them as needed. Dental health is also important; ensure regular dental check-ups and consider dental care products to help maintain their oral hygiene.

## *Illness and Injury Prevention*

Preventing illness and injury is crucial for maintaining the health and well-being of your aging Ragdoll. Proactive measures can help minimize risks and manage any emerging health issues effectively.

### *Regular Veterinary Visits*

Regular veterinary visits are key to detecting and addressing health issues early. Schedule comprehensive check-ups to monitor for common age-related conditions, such as kidney disease, diabetes, and arthritis. Your veterinarian can perform diagnostic tests, such as blood work and urinalysis, to assess your Ragdoll's internal health and catch any potential problems before they become serious.

### *Home Safety*

Make your home safe for your senior Ragdoll by reducing hazards that could lead to injury. Ensure that your home is free of obstacles that could cause your cat to trip or fall. Use non-slip mats on slippery surfaces and provide sturdy ramps or steps to assist with climbing. Keep toxic substances, such as certain plants and chemicals, out of reach to prevent accidental ingestion.

### *Preventative Measures*

Preventative measures, such as maintaining a healthy weight and providing joint supplements, can help reduce the risk of common age-related conditions. Monitor your Ragdoll's weight and adjust their diet and exercise as needed to prevent obesity. Joint supplements and arthritis medications, as recommended by your veterinarian, can help manage joint pain and improve mobility.

### *Vaccinations and Parasite Control*
Keep your Ragdoll up-to-date on vaccinations and parasite control. Even senior cats need protection against common diseases and parasites. Discuss with your veterinarian the appropriate vaccination schedule and any additional preventative measures needed based on your cat's health and lifestyle. Regular flea and tick prevention can also help protect your Ragdoll from external parasites and related health issues.

## *Senior Cat Nutrition*

Proper nutrition is vital for supporting the health and well-being of your aging Ragdoll. Adjusting their diet to meet their specific needs can help manage age-related changes and maintain their quality of life.

### *Nutritional Needs*
Senior cats have different nutritional needs compared to younger cats. They may require a diet that is lower in calories to prevent weight gain and easier to digest. Look for senior cat food formulations that provide balanced nutrition, including high-quality protein, vitamins, and minerals. Senior cat foods often contain added nutrients to support joint health, cognitive function, and overall vitality.

### *Hydration*
Adequate hydration is essential for senior cats, as they are more prone to dehydration and kidney issues. Ensure your Ragdoll has access to fresh, clean water at all times. Consider incorporating wet food into their diet to increase their water intake. Some senior cats may benefit from specially formulated diets that include higher moisture content to support urinary and kidney health.

## *Monitoring and Adjustments*

Monitor your Ragdoll's weight and body condition regularly and adjust their diet as needed. Weight loss or gain can indicate underlying health issues or the need for dietary adjustments. Consult with your veterinarian to develop a personalized nutrition plan that addresses your cat's specific health needs and preferences.

## **Special Dietary Considerations**

Certain health conditions may require specialized diets. For example, cats with kidney disease may benefit from a low-protein, low-phosphorus diet, while those with diabetes may need a high-fiber, low-carbohydrate diet. Work with your veterinarian to identify any special dietary needs and select appropriate food options that support your Ragdoll's health. Caring for an aging Ragdoll involves understanding and addressing their evolving needs. By providing appropriate care, monitoring their health, and making necessary adjustments, you can help ensure your senior cat enjoys a comfortable and fulfilling life in their later years.

# CHAPTER 15

# WHEN IT'S TIME TO SAY GOODBYE

## When to Say Goodbye

Deciding when to say goodbye to a beloved Ragdoll cat is one of the most challenging aspects of pet ownership. This decision involves assessing your cat's quality of life and considering both physical and emotional factors.

### *Assessing Quality of Life*

A key factor in deciding when to say goodbye is evaluating your cat's quality of life. Consider their overall comfort and happiness. Look for signs of pain, discomfort, or distress, such as difficulty breathing, persistent pain despite medication, severe mobility issues, or significant changes in appetite and behavior.

### *Veterinary Input*

Consult your veterinarian to get a professional assessment of your cat's condition. Your vet can help determine if your Ragdoll is suffering from an illness or condition that cannot be managed effectively and discuss their prognosis. They can also provide guidance on whether your cat's quality of life has deteriorated to the point where euthanasia might be the most humane option.

### *Personal Observations*

Reflect on your own observations and interactions with your cat. Consider their daily activities and how they are handling routine tasks. Are they still enjoying their favorite activities, or have they lost interest in things they once loved? Assessing these aspects can provide valuable insight into their overall well-being.

### *Emotional Readiness*

Understand that making the decision to say goodbye is an emotional process. It is important to balance your emotional attachment with your cat's welfare. Seek support from friends, family, or pet loss support groups to help you navigate this difficult time. Remember, your primary concern should be your cat's comfort and well-being.

## *The Euthanasia Process*

Euthanasia is a compassionate choice that can relieve suffering and ensure a peaceful end for your Ragdoll cat. Understanding the process can help you prepare and make the experience as gentle as possible for both you and your cat.

### *In-Home vs. Veterinary Clinic*

Euthanasia can be performed at home or in a veterinary clinic. In-home euthanasia allows your cat to pass away in a familiar and comforting environment. Many veterinary practices offer this service, and it can be beneficial for reducing stress for both you and your cat. Alternatively, a veterinary clinic provides a controlled environment and may offer additional support services.

### *The Procedure*

The euthanasia procedure typically involves

administering a sedative to help your cat relax and become comfortable. Once your cat is calm, the veterinarian will administer a euthanasia solution, usually through an injection. This solution is a painless, overdose of anesthetics that causes your cat to fall asleep and then pass away peacefully. Your veterinarian will guide you through the process and ensure that it is handled with compassion and respect.

### *Supporting Your Cat*
During the procedure, offer comfort to your cat by speaking softly and gently petting them if desired. Your presence and soothing touch can provide reassurance and help your cat feel at ease. If you choose in-home euthanasia, you can create a calming atmosphere with familiar items, such as your cat's favorite blanket or toys.

### *Making the Decision*
Deciding to proceed with euthanasia can be difficult. Allow yourself time to consider your options and discuss them with your veterinarian. They can provide additional insights and answer any questions you may have about the process.

Ultimately, your decision should prioritize your cat's comfort and minimize their suffering.

## *Final Arrangements*

After the decision has been made and your cat has passed away, you will need to make final arrangements. These arrangements can include decisions about handling your cat's remains and commemorating their life.

### **Handling the Remains**
You will need to decide how you would like to handle your cat's remains. Options typically include burial or cremation. If you choose burial, check local regulations regarding pet burials to ensure compliance with any legal requirements. You may also opt for cremation, which can be arranged through your veterinary clinic or a pet cremation service. Many services offer options for private cremation, which allows you to keep your cat's ashes in a memorial urn.

### **Commemorative Options**
Consider ways to commemorate your cat's life

and honor their memory. This can include creating a memorial, such as a plaque, garden, or photo album. Some pet owners choose to plant a tree or flower in their cat's honor. Personalizing a memorial can provide comfort and a lasting tribute to the bond you shared.

### *Managing the Logistics*

Your veterinarian or pet cremation service can assist with the logistics of handling your cat's remains. They can provide guidance on the process and help ensure that all arrangements are handled with care and respect. Take the time you need to make decisions that feel right for you and your family.

## *Grieving Your Loss*

Grieving the loss of your Ragdoll cat is a natural and important process. Allowing yourself to grieve and seek support can help you navigate the emotional impact of saying goodbye.

### *Emotional Response*

It is normal to experience a range of emotions

following the loss of a pet. You may feel sadness, anger, guilt, or even relief. Each person's grieving process is unique, and there is no right or wrong way to feel. Allow yourself to experience these emotions and seek support if needed.

### *Support Systems*

Reach out to friends, family, or support groups who understand the bond between pets and their owners. Talking about your feelings and sharing memories of your cat can provide comfort and help you process your grief. Pet loss support groups, both online and in-person, can offer additional understanding and encouragement during this time.

### *Memorializing Your Pet*

Creating a memorial for your cat can be a meaningful way to honor their memory and celebrate the joy they brought into your life. Consider creating a scrapbook, writing a letter, or making a donation to an animal charity in your cat's name. These activities can help you find closure and keep the positive memories of your Ragdoll alive.

### *Self-Care*
Take care of yourself during the grieving process. Ensure you are eating well, getting enough rest, and engaging in activities that bring you comfort and joy. Grieving can be physically and emotionally draining, so it is important to practice self-care and give yourself time to heal.

### *Moving Forward*
As time passes, you may find it easier to remember the happy moments you shared with your Ragdoll and appreciate the positive impact they had on your life. Moving forward does not mean forgetting your cat but rather cherishing their memory while allowing yourself to heal and eventually consider welcoming a new pet into your life if that feels right for you.

Saying goodbye to a beloved Ragdoll cat is a profound and emotional experience. By understanding the process, making thoughtful arrangements, and allowing yourself to grieve, you can navigate this difficult time with compassion and respect for both your cat and yourself.

# *CONCLUSION*

As we come to the end of this comprehensive guide on Ragdoll cats, it's clear that these unique and wonderful felines hold a special place in the hearts of cat lovers around the world. Ragdolls are not just pets; they are companions that bring immense joy, love, and comfort to their owners. This book has aimed to provide you with all the essential information needed to raise, care for, and understand your Ragdoll cat, ensuring a harmonious and fulfilling relationship that can last for many years.

In conclusion, Ragdoll cats are truly exceptional animals that bring warmth and happiness to any home. By choosing to share your life with a Ragdoll, you are embarking on a journey filled with rewarding experiences and a bond that will enrich your life in countless ways. May this book serve as a valuable companion in your journey, helping you to provide the best care and ensuring that you and your Ragdoll enjoy many happy years together.

**THE END**